The Ultimate Guide to Handling Every Disagreement Every Time

Okay, let's get started!

Dr. Robyn Odegaard

The Ultimate Guide to Handling Every Disagreement Every Time

ISBN 978-0-9846581-1-4

Disclaimer

This book is designed to provide information in regard to the subject matter covered. It is sold or provided with the understanding that the publisher, author, editor, and/or sponsor shall not be held liable in any degree for any loss or injury due to any omission, error, misprinting, or ambiguity. The publisher, author, and editor disclaim any personal liability, directly or indirectly, for advice or information presented within.

Published by Champion Performance Development

www.ChampPerformance.com

Edited by Scott Morgan
www.write-hook.com

Cover Art by Russell Bruzzano
www.rgbdesigngroup.com

Book Design by Russell Bruzzano
www.rgbdesigngroup.com

Printed in the United States of America

Praise for Dr. Robyn Odegaard

"Dr. Odegaard worked with me to create some simple, but very effective strategies to improve our effectiveness. Without Dr. Odegaard's keen insights and highly practical suggestions, I am certain our company would not have gotten off to a great start. I would recommend her to any organization, large or small, that is interested in creating an environment that leads to maximum performance."

Bill Howard, CEO – CoughCo

"The skills Doc Robyn provides allow people to unlock their potential through great teamwork. Professionals who use Doc Robyn's skills definitely have less drama and make better use of their potential."

James Malinchack, Featured on ABC's hit TV Show "Secret Millionaire" and Founder – www.BigMoneySpeaker.com

"I have used Dr. Robyn Odegaard's techniques to successfully negotiate with clients, to propose winning alternatives to my former boss, to eliminate tasks that don't add value to my business and to maintain my dignity when a client behaved in a manner that was undesirable to me.

Listening for Communication Fingerprints™ helps me to decide whether to welcome clients and vendors into our business ecosystem and to know how I can help them to reach their potential."

Jaime Campbell, CFO – Tier One Services

Contents

1 The Foundation to Every Disagreement You've Ever Had

The Problem and the Solution in 118 Words:

Why disagreements and misunderstandings happen and what to do about them is fundamentally misunderstood. Columbia University did a study that showed 80 percent of adults will *not* engage in conflict resolution without outside help. Even when we are willing to do so, there is a huge disconnect between how we present our case and how it is heard by the other person. Your most valuable information is being lost between leaving your mouth and being processed by the other person's brain.

You need to understand why this discrepancy occurs and how to overcome it in order to gain influence, freedom, success, profit and, most importantly, happiness by successfully handling every disagreement every time. This book shows you how.

I Was Not Born Good at Conflict Resolution

I am internationally known as a conflict resolution expert. I give keynote presentations and create workshops that show people how to use Productive Conflict™ (how to get all the cards on the table and pick the best hand – more on that later) for a living. And I am good at it.

From the outside, the reason for my success seems simple: I spent a lot of time in school and have fancy initials in front of my name. But that isn't what makes me good at teaching conflict resolution. What makes me good is, I used to be really, really lousy at it. If there was a mistake to be made, toes to step on or a way to put my foot in my mouth, I have done it.

It turns out that effective conflict resolution is not something you are innately good or bad at. It is a very learnable skill. You only need to understand why what you're doing now doesn't work and establish a method to handle things differently. Better method, better results. Better results, more business. More business, more money. Better results, better relationships. Better relationships, greater happiness.

How I Handled a Power Play

A few weeks ago I requested a meeting with a vendor to discuss lack of performance. I provided him with multiple days and times, a total of 14 hours that would work for me, my CFO and my business manager. The vendor wrote back saying none of those times worked for him and offering *one* 45-minute slot.

Clearly this was a power play to either force me not to have my team members present or to not have the meeting at all.

First, there is something you need to know about this vendor: He is a narcissist. That means that his Communication Fingerprint™ (how he uses language and what words mean to him – more about that in a bit) allows him to do whatever it takes to get his way. There is no boundary he won't cross. He will yell, scream, berate, lie, interrupt, cry and even threaten to sue if it serves his purpose. He has the ability to make people question their own sanity by staunchly defending something that didn't actually happen (did I mention he will lie?).

> **❝**Better method, better results. Better results, more business. More business, more money. Better results, better relationships. Better relationships, greater happiness. **❞**

I had three options:

1. Engage in his power game and push back (counterproductive)
2. Call him out (no gain to me)
3. Have a conversation with my team to acknowledge his power play and call his bluff

I went with the third choice. We adjusted our schedules to meet at the time he offered.

He then moved on to Power Play No. 2: he called me directly. Fortunately I was not available when he called and he had to leave a voicemail. He wanted to clarify the objective of the meeting so that he could be prepared. I answered via email, so that we could speak with him as a team during the scheduled meeting, rather than engaging with him one-on-one over the phone.

When we finally met with the vendor, as a team, the conversation was tense and at times threatened to escalate into a shouting match. Fortunately, because I understand how the Communication Corridor™ (how words are processed through the brain and heard differently than how they were said – more on that later) works, I was able to manage the emotional balance of the meeting, express what I needed to say, listen to where he stood on the problem and end the meeting without things degrading into a verbal sparring match.

As you will see, by understanding why and how conversations disintegrate into confrontations that stalemate and by knowing how to keep your cool, make the other person feel heard and make your point, you too can be a master of handling every disagreement, every time.

The Need for a New Approach

If ever there were a time when learning to use conflict resolution effectively could make a huge positive difference in life, it is now. Vendors are less responsive, customers are more demanding and competition is more intense than ever. There is so much advice out there, like "Stand your ground," "Negotiate for what you're worth" and "Don't let people steamroll you," but that's like a football commentator saying, "To win this game they need to score more points than their opponent." Really? Wow, am I glad someone pointed that out! If you are like me, you know *what* you need to do; the question is *how* to do it.

I knew I didn't need or want to be tougher, meaner or a bigger bully to get what I needed from vendors, provide my clients with outstanding service and outpace my competition while being happier and less stressed. There had to be a better way. What you will see in the following pages is that most of the time and energy you waste on disagreements and unresolved conflict isn't your fault nor even the other person's fault. We don't handle conflict well because our brains are foundationally hardwired to keep us alive. Your brain can't tell the difference between an emotional, verbal, psychological or physical threat. Great if you are living in the Serengeti and at risk of being eaten by a lion. Not so good when your heart pounds and your palms sweat whenever a client gets angry. The situation is made worse by how we are taught to communicate and what we believe about how language is used. I realized I needed to understand these flaws and learn how to work around them if I wanted to be able to limit the damage caused to my business and personal relationships by disagreement and negative, unresolved conflict.

Our DNA is Not Helpful!

Some really smart people who study neuroscience tell us that our brain is segmented into three general sections: the Primitive brain, the Mid-brain and the Neocortex. I call them the Caveman Brain, the Emotional Brain and the Logical Brain. Our first challenge in handling disagreements comes with how information is processed as it flows into, through and out of this Communication Corridor™. (Figure 1.1)

The Caveman Brain

This part of your brain is interested only in your survival. It wants to know things like, is my heart beating, am I getting enough oxygen,

5

do I need to run away (flight) and do I need to fight for my life? The Caveman Brain is the first stop for any information coming into the brain. If that information is a disagreement, the Caveman wants to know, what do I need to do to survive this? Any information it passes along to the Emotional Brain will be truncated to fit into this very tiny view of the world. Everything else is irrelevant.

> **❝Your brain can't tell the difference between an emotional, verbal, psychological or physical threat. Great if you are living in the Serengeti and at risk of being eaten by a lion. Not so good when your heart pounds and your palms sweat whenever a client gets angry. ❞**

The Emotional Brain

This midsection of our brain manages our social knowledge and interaction and adds feelings and meaning. Not the words (i.e., angry, sad, frustrated, etc.); just the actual raw emotion. People who have high emotional intelligence are able to use a lot of the information this part of their brain creates. This part of the brain doesn't ask questions or interpret information. It only supplies context to the abbreviated data it is given by the Caveman Brain (I provide an example in a minute).

The Logical Brain

Finally, we reach the processing center of the brain, where problem-solving, logic, language and all higher thought take place; where the pinnacle of the human brain, the frontal cortex, reigns supreme.

6

Information is gathered and decisions are made with lightning speed. It really is a marvel how efficiently the frontal cortex processes and spits out data. Except there are two flaws: One – this part of the brain isn't fully developed until we are about 22 years old (consider that the next time you are working with a high school or college-aged person); and Two – all of the information it receives is first filtered through the Caveman Brain (paring down everything not related to survival) and the Emotional Brain (adding context that may or may not be relevant).

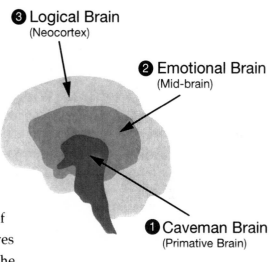

❸ Logical Brain
(Neocortex)

❷ Emotional Brain
(Mid-brain)

❶ Caveman Brain
(Primative Brain)

Figure 1.1 Communication Corridor™

Consider this example:

You are walking down the street. A car passes you and you hear a very loud explosion sound.

Caveman Brain: *"We are under attack! Increase heart rate, increase oxygen intake, tense muscles. Do I fight or run?!?!"*

Emotional Brain: *"Strangers in unknown vehicle + loud scary noise = terror!"* (Flood the Logical Brain with neurotransmitters.)

Logical Brain: *"Everybody stand down. The car just backfired. There is no threat."*

7

All of this happens in a split second and that is a good thing. If the situation was life threatening (the car was coming straight at you) you would be physically prepared to take immediate action to survive.

In the context of a disagreement:

You receive an email from a vendor saying that they understand they didn't meet your service expectations. But if you look at the fine print on the contract, they did meet their contractual obligations and no, they will not be refunding any of the $50,000 you invested with them. Thank you for your business.

Caveman Brain: *"We are under attack! Increase heart rate, increase oxygen intake, tense muscles. Do I fight or run?!?!"* (Remember, this part of the brain can't tell the difference between a physical, psychological, emotional or verbal attack. They all look and feel exactly the same.)

Emotional Brain: *"We trusted this vendor, they promised to deliver and we spent a lot of money. That isn't fair!"* (Flood the Logical Brain with neurotransmitters.)

Now the Logical Brain has to make a choice:

One – *"I am angry, fire off a email threatening to sue!"*

Two – *"Okay, breathe* (allowing the neurotransmitters to recede). *We need to look at the contract, see what our options are and move forward in a logical fashion."*

When you say something and immediately regret it, your Emotional Brain has hijacked your Logical Brain. If you are logically explaining something to someone and they keep saying, "Yeah, but…," You are likely confusing the situation with the facts. Their Emotional Brain is flooding their Logical Brain with neurotransmitters and your logic isn't being processed.

The Male and Female Brain are Different

When I was in grade school I once heard my Dad (who was a high school teacher and knew *everything*) say, "Boys are so easy. They will just get into a fistfight and get it over with. Girls will hold a grudge for twenty years." If you have heard me speak, you know I took that information to heart and got into a fistfight at school. Let's just say it didn't get things "over with" like I had hoped.

But at a certain level, Dad was on to something. The Emotional Brain of a man interprets incoming information differently than that of a woman. And how the Logical Brain acts on that information is different. What you might not know is, it used to be a matter of survival. Let's think about what was important when we were living in caves, hunting with sticks and cooking over an open pit.

What Matters to a Caveman

A caveman had two jobs: hunt for food and protect his family. In order to do both successfully he needed to be strong and healthy. His biggest fear was not being able to do these jobs. If you wanted to convince a caveman to do things your way, threatening or actually injuring him physically was your best bet. When a caveman was beaten, he would submit to the leader and fall in line in order continue to be one of the winners. That is, of course, until he saw a chance to be the leader himself. Then another fight would ensue. Men have a very "king of the jungle" way of looking at hierarchy.

We still see this behavior very prominently on professional sports teams. When arguments get heated, they escalate to blows pretty quickly, even though there are penalties for fighting. A man's dominance is tested when he goes head-to-head with another man (think about boxing or MMA fighting). There is always a certain "pecking order" within men's teams.

In boardrooms disagreements rarely come to blows. But we still see men displaying their dominance in social ways: biggest house, prettiest wife, fanciest car, the most extravagant vacation, boasting about running the project with the biggest budget, having the largest corner office. The list is endless. You will even see men resort to office politics and drama to assert their power once bragging and other displays don't get them what they want. A man's Emotional Brain processes information through the "How do I become and stay the leader of this group?" filter before it passes anything along to the Logical Brain.

Women do Things Differently

Now let's think about what a cavewoman's day might look like. These are a few of the things she would need to do: cook, clean, have children, raise children, make clothes, gather food, care for the sick, find firewood, make pottery, fetch water and anything else that needs to be done around the cave. She certainly isn't going to do all that work herself. She needs help from the other women in the cave complex. If she gets into a disagreement with another woman, injuring her physically creates one more person to take care of and two less hands to do any work. That would be counterproductive. So instead she is going to try to convince the group that the other woman is bad and push to exclude her from the group. However, the other woman isn't going to go quietly. She is going to try to push the first woman out of the group in return.

If you have ever watched any reality TV you have seen this happen. A group will end up with two sides and a middle, all bickering, gossiping and spreading rumors about each other. Only in extreme cases will things come to blows. In a professional setting and on women's teams, disagreements are met with office politics and drama. A woman's Emotional Brain uses the "How do I stay a member of this group while pushing out my rival?" filter as information flows to the Logical Brain. Women's teams are more likely to have cliques than a specific pecking order.

The next time you are in a meeting or group setting, take a moment to think about how the power in the room is decided. It is interesting to observe. What you will find is that men tend to view things from a He-who-wins-gets-his-way-and-he-who-loses-shuts-up-and-lines-up mentality. Women are more likely to be working to get the group to move in a specific direction together.

Another Way Men and Women are Different

There is one more piece of the social puzzle we need to consider. Up until the last couple of decades (and still in many cultures), women were dependent on men for a roof over their head and food on their table. This dependence created a risk to survival. If a man became angry he could decide to remove his support, thus leaving the woman without a way to provide for herself. With that risk it would be prudent for a woman to avoid conflict and not aggressively pursue her thoughts and ideas. The hundreds of years of training young women to defer to men in order to ensure their survival (and the survival of their children) still affects how men and women interact today.

Thought I Was Good to Go

Once I understood how the Communication Corridor™ filtered language and how men and women approached conflict from different places I thought I was ready to handle any disagreements that came my way. Then I learned about my Communication Fingerprint™, the Communication Myth™ and why the Communication Golden Rule™ is failing us.

In the pages ahead I will show you how to become aware of your individual Communication Fingerprint™, how the Communication Myth™ creates misunderstanding and how to avoid it and why you should stop using the Communication Golden Rule™. Plus loads of tips, tricks and skills you can use to achieve more from every conversation, handle every disagreement and have less negative conflict every day. DR

2 We All Have a Unique Communication Fingerprint™

Each one of us has a unique and interesting life story. As part of that story we learn to communicate and handle disagreements from the people around us. As children we learn from our parents, our teachers and our friends. We start to understand how the meaning of a word can be altered by inflection and context. What is funny, rude or sarcastic becomes clearer. Each interaction hones our skill in understanding the 95 percent of communication that is based on tone, body language or facial expression and has nothing to do with the actual words spoken.

An Example from My Childhood

When I was a preteen, I was making myself a sandwich at the kitchen table when my four-year-old brother asked who the sandwich was for. I responded, rather sarcastically, "yours truly." I thought I had clearly communicated that I was making it for myself; however, when I took the first bite, he started to cry, claiming that I was eating *his* sandwich.

I explained to Dad that I had said the sandwich was for me. Dad pointed out that a four-year-old did not understand that "yours truly" meant "me," no matter how sarcastically I said it. I had to hand over the sandwich to my brother and make myself another one. I learned that I needed to be more straightforward when speaking to my younger siblings (and to make more than one sandwich at a time).

A few years later, I was visiting my aunt and was told to make myself a sandwich. I laid out enough bread for everyone in the room and started asking what everyone wanted. My aunt and uncle laughed at me because to me "make yourself a sandwich" meant "make sandwiches for everyone." The

> **❝** *The more diverse the experiences on the team are, the greater the differences in their Communication Fingerprints™ will be, and the greater their risk of miscommunication.* **❞**

Communication Fingerprint™ I had learned at home did not translate to my aunt's house. (You might be interested to know that I will still ask if anyone wants a sandwich if I am making one for myself. The Communication Fingerprint™ we learn in childhood is deeply ingrained.)

· · · · · · · · ·

Since each of our lives is unique, everyone develops a distinctive, ingrained style of communication – their individual Communication Fingerprint™. People from the same family tend to communicate in a similar fashion. Individuals from the same region of the country communicate in a similar style and people from the same country are likely to understand each other better than those from another country, even if they speak the same language. On a team of only ten people, there are likely to be ten distinctly different styles and expectations of communication. The more diverse the experiences on the team are, the greater the differences in their Communication Fingerprints™ will be, and the greater their risk of miscommunication. No wonder we often struggle to get our points across to one another in a disagreement!

When I start working with an executive coaching client and when I do teambuilding workshops, one of the most important things I do is have people think about why they communicate the way they do. Since I am not sitting next to you to facilitate the conversation, the next best thing is to provide you with several of the conversation starters I use. I have included answers I have heard over the years to get you thinking. Consider the following, write notes in the space provided and reflect on how these events shaped how you use language and how you approach disagreements now. There are no right or wrong answers and I will not be labeling you at the end. This is about you growing in the understanding of how your Caveman Brain, Emotional Brain and Logical Brain (the Communication Corridor™) work together to create your Individual Communication Fingerprint™. The more honest you can be with yourself, the more you will get out of the exercise.

Determining your Individual Communication Fingerprint™

When you were a child:

- How did your parents and other adults in your home(s) speak to each other?
  - o They didn't really speak
  - o Always yelling
  - o Calm, logical conversations
  - o Only behind closed doors
  - o One talked the other only listened
  - o One dominant person always got his/her way

  _____

  _____

  _____

- When you disagreed with your parents, how was it handled?
  - o I was allowed to state my case even if I didn't get my way
  - o I would scream or throw a tantrum and usually got my way
  - o I was told what to do. If I said anything I was "talking back"
  - o Disagreement was met with corporal punishment
  - o My parents didn't really care what I did so we didn't disagree

  _____

  _____

  _____

- How were (and even are) family meals?
  - o Loud, everyone always talking over each other
  - o A few conversations going. People usually talked to the people sitting near them

16

o One person talked (always the same person?), everyone else listened

o The TV was on. We didn't usually talk unless it was about what was on TV

o Family meals? We rarely ate together

_____

_____

_____

• When I played with my friends

　o I decided what we would play and who could play with us

　o I was happy to follow the lead on whatever was going on

　o I mostly played by myself

　o Being the leader or the follower depended on the group I was with

_____

_____

_____

• When someone did something I didn't like I

　o Cried and/or went to my room alone

　o Defended myself using my fists

　o Got my friends involved and ganged up on them

　o Talked to my friends about what an awful person he/she was

　o Waited and looked for a way to get them back

_____

_____

_____

- In school I
  - o Succeeded easily and never had to ask questions
  - o Mostly succeeded but it was work and I asked a lot of questions
  - o Really struggled. School was hard for me and I often felt stupid
  - o I didn't really care about school

  _____

  _____

  _____

- In organized groups, sports teams, clubs or camps my leaders/coaches
  - o Did a lot of yelling
  - o Expected me to just "get it" without much explanation
  - o Really went out of their way to help me understand
  - o I didn't participate in group activities

  _____

  _____

  _____

As an adult:
- Other people say this about my sense of humor:
  - o Only my family really gets it
  - o Everyone thinks I am hysterical
  - o I am a great story teller and am seen as generally funny
  - o People don't think of me as funny

  _____

  _____

  _____

- When I am stressed or unhappy I expect my friends to:
  - Know what I need and give it to me
  - Leave me alone and let me work through it
  - Ask what I need
  - My friends don't notice when I'm stressed

_____

_____

_____

- I am motivated by:
  - Looming deadlines
  - People praising my accomplishments
  - Physical rewards such as money or gifts
  - A sense of a job well done
  - Guilt for not doing what I am supposed to do
  - Someone yelling at me to give my all

_____

_____

_____

- I motivate others by:
  - Setting clear expectations and holding others accountable
  - Being encouraging
  - Telling them what I need and expecting it to happen
  - Providing physical rewards such as money or gifts
  - Yelling encouragement

_____

_____

- When I have to explain the same thing more than once I:
  - o Get frustrated that they don't get it
  - o Dumb it down for them
  - o Just keep going through it until they get it
  - o Ask them what they don't understand

  _____

  _____

  _____

- When someone annoys me or hurts my feelings I usually:
  - o Ignore it. It's not worth the energy to say something
  - o Speak up right away. They can't fix it if I don't tell them what is wrong
  - o Hint at what is wrong until they figure it out
  - o Give them the cold shoulder until I feel better

  _____

  _____

  _____

- I think practical jokes are:
  - o Great fun, I don't know why everyone doesn't love them
  - o Awful! You shouldn't treat other people like idiots
  - o Funny as long as they are being pulled on someone else

  _____

  _____

  _____

I wish I could be sitting next to you having a conversation about the components of your individual Communication Fingerprint™. Everything you wrote down is a piece of the puzzle of how you unconsciously use and process language; what you say, how you say it, what you mean when you say it and what you hear when others speak to you. Each element was created because it served a purpose at that time. Everyone I have ever worked with retains a certain amount of their fingerprint from childhood, even though it no longer really works for them. They just never realized how badly it was limiting their success. Fortunately, our Communication Fingerprints™ are malleable. Now that you are more aware of what your Communication Fingerprint™ looks like, you are ready to make changes to it to better suit where your life is now as opposed to where you were when you were five years old.

> **❝***Everything you wrote down is a piece of the puzzle of how you unconsciously use and process language; what you say, how you say it, what you mean when you say it and what you hear when others speak to you.* **❞**

But before we move on to specific skills, there are two more pieces to the challenges we face when communicating and resolving disagreements on a daily basis: The Communication Myth™ and the failure of the Communication Golden Rule™.

The Communication Myth™

The best way I have found to explain the Communication Myth™ is to compare it to driving. Studies have shown that about 80 percent of adults consider themselves better-than-average drivers. Which is why there are bumper stickers that say "Why am I the only person on the planet who can drive?" and why it is incredibly funny to see that bumper sticker on a car that is upside-down on the road. (Yes, I really have a picture like that in my presentations.)

Similarly, if you look at LinkedIn profiles or peruse through a stack of résumés, you will find many of them say something like "Excellent oral and written communication."

A great example is a conversation I had with someone who was referred to me as a potential client by his brother and business partner because they were on the verge of dissolving their partnership and going their separate ways. The younger brother wanted them both to work with me to address what he viewed as a major communication problem. I sat in a noisy coffee shop and listened to the older brother give a long list of reasons why his brother and partner was wrong and if he would just stop being so stubborn and do things the "right" way (i.e., his way) their business would be wildly successful. He summed up the entire problem with their partnership in three sentences, *"I am an excellent communicator. I always say **exactly** what I mean. I can't help it if other people don't understand me."*

· · · · · · · · ·

The problem with this thought process is, it leads us to believe that miscommunication and disagreement are always the other

22

person's fault. Each of us has the unconscious idea that we are above average at communicating our needs and desires. Therefore, any problems that arise due to miscommunication must be the other person's fault.

So we have our Caveman Brain and our Emotional Brain hijacking our Logical Brain, a unique way of using and interpreting language once it does reach our Logical Brain, and we think we are above average at communication. What else could possibly be in the way of our successfully dealing with disagreements?

Well, there is just one more thing... The failure of the Communication Golden Rule™

The Communication Golden Rule™

We all know the Golden Rule: "Treat others the way you want to be treated." It seems like a pretty straightforward way of saying, everyone play nice and we'll get along just fine. There is one, big, glaring problem, however. The Golden Rule assumes we are all the same, want the same things, find the same things funny and communicate the same way.

My best friend of almost twenty years, Carmen, and I ran into this problem early on in our budding friendship:

> **❝Each of us has the unconscious idea that we are above average at communicating our needs and desires. ❞**

She called me one morning and in a very solemn voice said, "*I have something I need to tell you.*" Of course my response was that she could tell me anything. She

23

proceeded to tell me that her brother had just told the family he was gay and that her parents were not taking it well. We talked at length about the challenges of the situation and how we could best be supportive to her brother and to help her parents accept the situation. It was an emotionally intense conversation for me, interrupted by Carmen telling me that her sister was calling on the other line and she would call me back.

After we hung up, I continued to think about her brother and how his revelation might affect her family. Five minutes later she called me back, laughing hysterically, and said, *"April Fool's! I was just pulling your leg! He's not gay!"*

I was completely devastated. I do not like practical jokes. I certainly do not like to be made fool of and I did not believe the emotionally charged subject of someone's sexuality should be a topic of fodder for April Fool's Day. After what seemed like forever, she stopped laughing and said, *"Oh, come on, lighten up. It's just a joke."* To which I responded, *"If I trust you enough that you could pull such a stunt, I would expect you to respect me enough not to"* and hung up the phone.

To this day Carmen, her husband and even her children believe practical jokes to be a fun and good-natured way for people who care about each other to interact. I have no doubt their other friends pull practical jokes on each other regularly to the delight of everyone involved. However, in treating me that way, grave damage could have been done to our friendship because I felt lied to and emotionally abused. The Golden Rule most certainly did not apply. (Don't worry, we talked through it and I would now trust her with my life.)

•••••••••

So our Logical Brain gets only part of the story, overlaid with emotion that may or may not be relevant. We use our "perfect" individual Communication Fingerprint™ to respond and we assume other people are like us. In other words, that they hear what we mean, not what they interpreted out of the words we use. The situation becomes frustrating and everyone keeps saying the same things, only louder. And then we wonder why misunderstandings and disagreements escalate. It is like using a Black Box of Hope™ (Figure 2.1) to talk to each other.

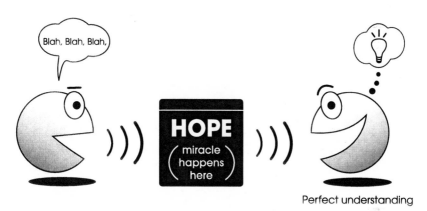

Figure 2.1 The Black Box Of Hope™

I used to use this method. I had the unconscious belief that if someone didn't agree with me they must not have heard me, so I repeated myself. Once I understood the four roadblocks to successful communication (Communication Corridor,™ Communication Fingerprint,™ Communication Myth,™ and Communication Golden Rule™) I realized I held the keys to handling every disagreement.

Now that you understand the stumbling blocks to effective conflict resolution you can use them as steppingstones to creating Productive

Conflict.™ Keep reading to learn the skills I share with executives, business owners and teams to help them achieve greatness by successfully handling every disagreement every time. **DR**

Thought Starters ( )

Do you think you are better than average at explaining what you need or want? Why or why not?

_____

_____

_____

Give an example of a time when you thought you made yourself clear and later realized what you thought you said was not what the other person heard.

_____

_____

_____

What do you think caused the misunderstanding?

_____

_____

_____

Continued!

3 We Need More Conflict in Our Lives!

I was sitting in a large, comfortable chair across a wide, shiny, dark, wooden table from a company owner/CEO. She had been in business for eight years and from the looks of things her business was doing well. But she was telling me about a couple of problems that were causing her profit margin to suffer:

One – Clients would engage her services and pay her substantial fee upfront. But then about two-thirds of the way through the project they would get distracted, start blowing off meetings and stop providing the information her team needed to wrap things up. She had multiple situations where employees were tied up babysitting a stalled project.

Two – A client had contracted her to work with his firm for a year to accomplish several different things. After the year was up, he reached out to her and she explained that their contract period had ended. He complained that he didn't realize the contract was only for a year and that this "one" thing didn't get done. She relented and said she would give him 30 more days. The conversation I was having with her was 90 days later and she was still working with him.

You would be surprised how often I am brought into businesses to address this exact problem - owners bending over backwards to appease their customers to the detriment of their bottom lines. I am all for great customer service, but letting your customers take advantage of you isn't a great plan either. That is where more conflict comes in. We all need to be better at saying, "I hear you. I understand your concern." *And* "That isn't going to be an option." That means being able to engage in what I call Productive Conflict™ – the ability to bring a concern out into the open, have a level-headed discussion (using the Logical Brain) about it and come up with a solution that doesn't make us feel like we have been taken advantage of.

Productive Conflict™

Productive Conflict™ occurs when two (or more) people who disagree get to state their case, have a discussion about the points on which they disagree, develop a solution and implement it. No screaming, no hurt feelings, no gossip, no misunderstandings and no drama.

Everyone dislikes conflict. There is nothing fun about it. It is uncomfortable, wrought with emotional landmines and risks that make our stomachs hurt. Most people avoid it; even to their own detriment. I have seen people dance around a problem, hint at what they want, stew when it doesn't happen and then explode. We expect other people to just *know* what we want and do what we think is fair or right. Unfortunately most of our customers are worried about their own best interest and if that means taking advantage of us, they are willing to do it.

How to Use Productive Conflict™

It is important to realize that most people have no idea how to have or manage a Productive Conflict™ conversation. Once you do, you are going to be responsible for stepping up to the plate and making it happen.

- **Notice that there is a problem that needs to be addressed.** Many of us are so skilled at avoiding conflict that we don't even realize we are doing it. It is just "good customer service." When something feels like it

> **❝***Productive Conflict™ occurs when two (or more) people who disagree get to state their case, have a discussion about the points on which they disagree, develop a solution and implement it.* **❞**

isn't right or isn't good for your business, don't ignore your "gut." That is your Emotional Brain trying to tell you to speak up.

- **Try not to have Productive Conflict™ conversations when clients first spring something on you.** Give yourself time to think about what the best answer is. Listen to their concerns; take notes if you need to. Make sure you understand exactly what their concerns are. Use active listening (more on how to do that in Chapter 8) statements like: "If I understand correctly, you are saying…" "Your main concern is…" Ask them what their "perfect" solution would be. Then let them know you need to think about it and schedule time to follow up.

> **❝Many of us are so skilled at avoiding conflict that we don't even realize we are doing it.❞**

- When you come back to the conversation, **know what your "perfect" solution is, where you are willing to compromise and what your deal-breakers are.** You are never so desperate for customers that allowing someone to steal your profit is the right answer (How does that benefit you?). Talk about your concerns using "I" statements. Be careful about using sentences that start with "you."

- **Discuss common ground, solutions and options.** Ask your customers where they see options for compromise. Realize that sometimes the only answer is being able to agree to disagree and go your separate ways. But it doesn't take yelling, screaming or cussing to get to that point.

- **Implement.** Once you reach agreement put the tough conversation behind you and move forward as a mutually beneficial team.

Conflict is never fun. But coming up with a solution and avoiding a major confrontation is very rewarding for you, your business and your clients. You will also get a reputation for being a great team player and collaborator if you are able to successfully use Productive Conflict™ and avoid the grudge matches that can so easily undermine your ability to succeed. Ultimately, clients who understand that you are looking for the option that is fair to both of you will respect you more. And those are the types of clients we all love to have!

Next up: I share some strategies that make disagreements worse. I bet you have seen or even used a few in your day! DR

Thought Starters ( )

What situations in your life could benefit from Productive Conflict™?

_____

_____

_____

How would it benefit you if those situations were resolved?

_____

_____

_____

What is keeping you from resolving them?

_____

_____

_____

Press on!

4 Disagreement Methods That Don't Work

The Volcano

I sat in stunned silence (which I will admit doesn't happen to me very often) and reread the email I had just received from a former client. I would quote it but the amount of %!*@&# that you would have to read would just be silly.

I had been working with this client for some time and we had reached the end of our contract. I had been paid and our final meeting had gone perfectly fine. So I was understandably shocked to receive his curse-laden email complaining about the terms of the contract we had signed six months before.

I picked up the phone to see if I could get some clarification.

Me: *Hey, Todd. I just saw your email from this morning....* (He interrupted me)

Todd: *Yeah, I'm pretty P.O.ed* (it wasn't that polite) *about our contract.*

Me: *Okay, I'm unclear why you're upset now that we're finished.*

Todd: (escalating) *I never liked the terms of our contract! I don't feel like I got what I wanted from our work!*

Me: *To help me understand the issue, let's start at the beginning. Why didn't you say something about it six months ago before we signed it or at our last meeting?*

Todd: *I didn't want to. I am NOT happy that you are unwilling to be flexible!*

Me: (still confused) *Okay, how would you....* (He interrupted me again)

Todd: (screaming) *You're *(&!<^# fired!* (and he slammed down the phone)

I pulled my ear piece out with a wince and looked at my phone more confused than when I had picked it up. I have never, before or since, been fired from a job that was complete.

·········

We are all guilty of using the Volcano method at some point. We know that something isn't right but we don't speak up. We might even tell ourselves it's fine, it's not a big deal or we'll just get over it. Rather than say or do anything about it, we push it down and ignore it, thinking it will go away.

Over time, the pressure builds. Eventually something - possibly even a "small" something - causes us to explode, spewing the hot lava of anger and frustration all over the unsuspecting target. One of the major issues with this method is the amount of time it takes to clean up. Not only does all the "stuff" that was packed down for so long have to be addressed, so do the hurt feelings and damage done by the explosion. It is much messier than if the issue had been addressed at the time it occurred.

> **"**I encourage you to ask yourself what is keeping you from addressing issues while they are still small.**"**

If you have a Volcano exploding on you, your best course of action is to put up your emotional shields and let them rant. Be cautious about letting your Caveman Brain or Emotional Brain jump into the conversation. It is a no-win until the Volcano is done spewing.

If you see yourself in the Volcano example, I encourage you to ask yourself what is keeping you from addressing issues while they are still small. What do you think causes you to wait until you are angry to say something?

The Packrat

I cringed in the passenger's seat as I heard the comment come out of my teammate's mouth. I knew Julie was sensitive about her driving. I had stuck my foot in my mouth over it before. I had even warned Becca that if she was going to ride with us we would need to leave early. Julie drove the speed limit, even in the left lane. It didn't matter if you were late, if she was backing up traffic, being flipped-off or if the world was ending. The law was the law and she didn't want a ticket. I waited. Would it be tears? Would she just turn the car around and make us even later by bringing us back to the office? I could tell by Julie's white knuckles that this wasn't going to be a comfortable ride. I turned and glared at Becca.

·········

The Packrat is similar to the Volcano in that issues are being ignored; however, it is different because pressure doesn't necessarily build up and things don't usually explode. Instead, this person packs trunks of emotional stuff and stashes them all over their emotional space. No one, including the person herself, really knows when they might bump into one of those trunks and spill the contents. Doing so can lead to a variety of responses, from tears to screaming to sullenness or depression. As a result, people who know Packrats feel like they need to walk on eggshells. If you just met a Packrat you will likely experience their emotional landmines very soon. With someone like this it often seems easier to just ignore issues and concerns rather than risk the disproportionate emotional response that is always a risk.

If you interact with a known Packrat on a regular basis you might try having a conversation with them to make the unconscious conscious. Talk to them about how it seems like things that should be non-issues set them off. Get them to talk about why they think that is and if they have any ideas to make the situation better. Of course, don't start this conversation when they are already upset about something. Do it when they are likely to be able to have a calm conversation.

If you see yourself in the Packrat example you can start to unpack some of those boxes by understanding where they are. If you aren't sure what your trigger points are, ask someone you trust. Can you think of what caused you to pack that baggage? It might be wise to talk to a professional who can help you uncover the emotions underlying your triggers.

The Solver

I was sitting in my office reading a report when I saw Debbie breeze past my office door. She made it about two steps and stopped, turned around, stopped again, turned back the way she was going, hesitated, then spun around, stuck her head around the door jam and said, "Oh hey, you're in. Great. Glad I caught you." She proceeded to plop herself down in a chair. "Did you hear…"

I put down the highlighter, took off my reading glasses and wondered if I should tell her I was too busy to listen to what I was sure was going to be a pat-myself-on-the-back story. Or was I going to take this opportunity to offer a bit of coaching. I let her continue.

"… Kurt made Grace cry, right in the lunch room yesterday. I decided I wasn't going to have that kind of drama happening on my watch so I sat them down and made them talk it out right there. I even had them hugging by the time I left."

She looked at me expectantly. Yep, coaching, coming right up.

• • • • • • • • •

A Solver is all about getting issues out in the open, particularly ones that have nothing to do with him. He will gladly mediate conversations about other people's issues. Sharing 'concerns' about other people under the guise of being worried about them and wanting to be helpful is common. This person will always be "in the know" about what is going on with whom. If you need the latest juicy gossip, he is your go-to person. The reality is, a Solver isn't actually solving anything—he is simply stirring the pot and fanning the flames of a firestorm. Additionally, it is very possible he is hiding concerns and issues about himself behind all the noise of trying to "help" everyone else.

If you have a Solver in your life you know how hard it is to get them to stop. If you say something they act hurt, as if you don't appreciate the great favor they are doing for you. Pull them aside and let them know you think it's great they want to help people and if you need their assistance, you will most certainly ask. However, it is important that they let you work through things on your own. Oh, and ask them not to share other people's business with you.

If you can hear yourself being a Solver I would encourage you to ask people if they would like your help before you give it.

Pollyanna

I had been brought in to work with a team of eight executives. Most of them understood that as a team they were struggling to provide their direct reports with clear direction. As a result their departments were arguing over resources, finger-pointing about mistakes and refusing to problem-solve together. The customer experience was seriously suffering.

There was one exception, Barry. I had spent a couple of hours trying to get to the bottom of how he managed his department. The other executives had complained about the "loosy-goosy" attitude of Barry's department and how the work that came out of it was a hodge-podge of some really great stuff and some out-of-left-field uselessness.

From Barry's point of view, everything was great. He didn't enforce the company dress code, went out for beers with his direct reports a couple of times a month and had the highest scores on the manager review survey. If there was a problem on the executive team it was that everyone else was way too uptight. "Loosen up! It's all good!" was Barry's mantra in life.

> **❝**_A team member who always looks at the world through rose-colored glasses will quickly find himself discounted, not taken seriously and ostracized by his teammates._**❞**

· · · · · · · · ·

Nothing is ever wrong here. The world is all sunshine and rainbows; no worries at all. A team member who always looks at the world through rose-colored glasses will quickly find himself discounted, not taken seriously and ostracized by his teammates. Even when he has good ideas, he will be ignored. Managers tend to love employees like this because they are easy to work with. Making them a "teacher's pet" will only deepen the gulf between them and their teammates. When they are placed in leadership roles they just want to be everybody's friend and figure the work will get done eventually. Being positive is great, as long as the person is willing to listen and address concerns when their _laissez-faire_ attitude isn't getting the work done.

41

Pollyannas can be one of the most frustrating types to work with because they are just so darn nice and positive but nothing ever gets done. I have found they can focus on and address a problem if they are forced to do so. It just requires strong motivation. Barry was on the verge of losing his job before he started to make changes and he eventually decided that the straight-laced corporate environment wasn't the right place for him.

If you see yourself in this story, find work you find fulfilling and that fits your personality. When your friends, family or teammates ask to engage you in a conversation about a problem, be careful about blowing them off with "It's not a big deal." Try to listen to what they have to say from their perspective.

> **"***A person who uses Toxic Churn believes things are horrible and getting worse. Poking old wounds is a specialty. Conflict is never over. Grudges are a given.***"**

Toxic Churn

My phone rang just as I was finishing dinner. I looked at the name on my caller ID and internally groaned. I knew the person calling only called when he needed 911-therapy; which lately seemed to be all the time. It is one thing when someone is paying me to listen to what ails them and wants help but this guy was from a pickup volleyball team I played on and was just calling to complain. He certainly wasn't interested in solutions. I knew that if I took this call I was going to get a very longwinded update about how badly he slept, how much his knee was bothering him, that his boyfriend was annoying, that his mother wasn't doing well and who on the team he was angry with now. After working a full day I didn't have the energy for this vampire and I let it go to voicemail.

·········

The opposite of Pollyanna, a person who uses Toxic Churn believes things are horrible and getting worse. Poking old wounds is a specialty. Conflict is never over. Grudges are a given. As an old Garth Brooks song puts it, "bury the hatchet, but leave the handle sticking out." Firestorming (whipping up a storm of gossip, backstabbing and cattiness) is great fun and complaining is the norm.

People who like to Toxic Churn are not likely to change without outside help. You can tell them you aren't interested in hearing it but you will likely have to repeat yourself ad nauseam. In the short-term you can avoid them. If this is someone you have to be around a lot you are going to want to read Chapter 11 to learn more about how to protect yourself from toxic people.

If you see yourself in the Toxic Churn example I would recommend having a conversation with a professional about depression. That level of negativity is not only toxic to everyone around you, it is bad for your personal health.

The Terminator

It was ten o'clock on a Saturday morning and I was already two hours into a contentious conference call about an outage that had one of our main databases offline. The call center was flooded with angry customer calls and our techs were struggling to find the problem. I already had my hands full facilitating the discussion involving multiple vendors to keep us on track to fix the situation when a very high-level executive arrived on the call and without so much as introducing himself, started screaming.

He wanted to know what had happened, why it wasn't fixed and who the blankety-blank-blank-blank was the idiot who was running this show anyway. Without even breathing, he said he was going to fire every person on the call and bring in some people who didn't have their head up their.... Well you can guess the rest.

I took a deep breath. I was the only person on the call he had the authority to fire and I was the "blankety-blank" he was looking for. Yay me.

● ● ● ● ● ● ● ● ●

The Terminator method is usually only tolerated from very high-level executives and business owners; people with a lot of power. And they only act that way when they are talking to people with less power. They try to take the easy way out of conflict. They will very publicly fire, penalize, remove from the project and otherwise punish anyone who doesn't do things their way. This creates a scared team of yes-men and yes-women. Everyone becomes afraid to make mistakes and they won't so much as think unless they are told which thoughts to have. Such a "leader" (I use the term loosely) might bring a project in on time and within budget, but top talent will not tolerate being treated this way for long.

If you are working for a Terminator, you are being abused. No job is worth that kind of treatment.

If you recognize yourself as a Terminator, I encourage you to address your anger issues.

The Kitchen-sinker

I had only stepped out of the meeting for five minutes. When I left they were having a productive discussion about the timeline and process flow of a new project. When I returned they seemed to be having an argument about which team was responsible for a delay in a project that had wrapped up several months ago. I was confused. How did they end up so far off topic so quickly?

....

Have you ever had a discussion with someone that escalated into a disagreement and the thing you end up fighting about has nothing to do with the original topic? I hear this complaint from all of my clients; from the twenty-something whose parents pay me to provide "life coaching" all the way up to the CEO who is

> **❝***If you are working for a Terminator you are being abused. No job is worth that kind of treatment.* **❞**

about to retire. I call it "Kitchen-sinking" because this person will emotionally throw everything into an argument including the kitchen sink. It is almost impossible to solve a problem with them because you can't remember what the problem was.

If you are having a discussion with a Kitchen-sinker, I highly recommend getting out a piece of paper (yes, an old fashion piece of paper). At the top, write down exactly what problem you are trying to solve. When they bring up something that isn't about that problem, let them know you can talk about that in a minute and write it down under the main issue. Then steer the conversation back to the topic at hand.

If you are a Kitchen-sinker, you might have trouble catching yourself doing it at first. Ask someone close to you if you think you might be guilty of it. If you find that your disagreements regularly end up off topic, use the piece of paper method I mentioned above.

When I share examples of conflict resolution styles that don't work, it really highlights for people how none of us are ever taught how to have a disagreement. We all just stumble through and hope we figure something out through the school of hard knocks. Fortunately, recognizing what doesn't work means you can get on the path to what does.

> **❝** *None of us are ever taught how to have a disagreement. We all just stumble through and hope we figure something out through the school of hard knocks.* **❞**

What if you could change how you looked at disagreements so that you could quickly and easily tell if a conversation was productive and likely to reach a resolution or just going to go in circles? The next chapter will give you those insights. DR

Thought Starters ( )

Which unproductive methods of conflict are you guilty of using?

_____

_____

_____

How old do you think you were when you learned to used that method?

_____

_____

_____

Do you think your use of those unproductive methods are helping or hurting your ability to resolve problems?

_____

_____

_____

5 A New Way to Think About Disagreements

Every disagreement can be broken down to two big pieces: the problem and the people. The problem, or the issue that needs to be solved, is what should be discussed. However, we usually end up talking about the person or people involved.

Think about the most recent argument you saw or heard. Were they using their Logical Brain to talk about a misunderstanding, an event or an action that led to their disagreement? I would wager no. They were probably talking about each other. "You did…" "Yeah but, you did…."

In order to effectively use Productive Conflict™ to reach a resolution it is important to recognize when a discussion, even a heated one, is about the problem and when it has become about the people involved. Which means being able to distinguish between *relationship conflict* and *informational conflict*.

Relationship Conflict

This type of conflict happens when the Logical Brain doesn't recognize that the feelings the Emotional Brain is sending are about the people, not the problem itself. Arguments will include words meant to tear down or damage the other person's character. You might hear things like "stupid," "dumb," "doesn't think," "cares only about himself," "isn't interested in the good of the team," "backstabbing" or other nasty opinions. These character judgments often include derogatory stories or examples meant to "prove" what the accuser is saying is true (and lead to kitchen-sinking). It is common for conversations that include relationship conflict to get off track and escalate quickly. They stop only when the parties are separated and do not result in a resolution.

> **❝**Respectful cognitive conflict improves trust and strengthens personal and professional bonds. **❞**

Relationship conflict accomplishes absolutely nothing. It creates defensiveness, hurt feelings and resentment. There is no upside to these types of arguments. No one can win and everyone will lose. Worse, relationship conflict masks the real problem. The undercurrent of anger and disrespect remains to boil over again the next time the parties interact.

Informational Conflict

In contrast, informational conflict (also called "cognitive conflict" by psychologists) is about the actual problem, topic or issue. The conversation originates in the Logical Brain and is about what happened and the feelings that exist because of it. Cognitive conflict is productive. There won't be accusations about someone's character or declarations as to why someone else is behaving a certain way. Disagreements of this type involve the *sharing of information*. There are lots of "I" statements: "I felt this way," "I observed this behavior," "This was my experience," "I had this reaction," "I would like to see this happen to solve the problem." Everyone owns their side of the conversation and the feelings they have rather than trying to tell someone else what they did or didn't do.

Informational conflict moves people toward resolution. As information about a problem is shared, understanding grows and *win-win solutions* can be discovered. Respectful cognitive conflict improves trust and strengthens personal and professional bonds.

To handle your next disagreement more effectively, reduce relationship conflict by eliminating character attacks and discuss informational differences by sharing where you stand and how you feel. If you can own your thoughts and feelings while listening to the thoughts and feelings of others, you will be able to discuss the problem rather than the person and reach a mutually acceptable resolution.

To help you identify the warning signs that you are engaging in relationship conflict there are five things you should *never* say in an argument. Learn what they are in the next chapter. DR

Thought Starters ❨❩

Consider your most recent disagreement: What percentage of the information exchanged was about the problem (informational) and how much was about the people (relational)?

_____

_____

_____

The next time you see a heated discussion on TV, notice if they are talking about the problem or the people. How do you think what you see on TV affects how you deal with disagreement?

_____

_____

_____

Do the people in your life (family, work, friends) use relationship or informational conflict?

_____

_____

_____

6 Five Things You Should *Never* Say in an Argument

I was sitting in a fancy restaurant having dinner with clients, trying to ignore the escalating tension in the booth next to us. Unfortunately (in this situation at least) I have very good hearing and am especially perceptive when it comes to emotional energy. Up until our salad plates had been cleared no one else at my table even noticed there was a fight brewing just over the divider. Then:

Him (not overly loud but with force and anger): *Now you are just making me angry.*

Her (raising her voice above his): *This is your fault! You shouldn't have put me in that situation. It wasn't fair…*

Him (interrupting and impatient): *That is just stupid! I didn't put you in a situation!*

Her (screaming over her shoulder as she stormed away from the table): *Forget it! You aren't listening to me anyway!*

My dinner companions sat in stunned silence until I said, "Sounds like they could use a conflict resolution expert. Too bad I'm booked solid tonight." The group chuckled and the tension at our table eased. I can't say the same for the abandoned man at the other table, who awkwardly paid the bill and followed in the direction of the departed woman. As our main course was served I thought, "Wow, they managed to use all five of the things you shouldn't say in an argument in one very public disagreement."

· · · · · · · · ·

Disagreements and even arguments are a normal part of being human. In fact, if two people never disagree, it is pretty likely that one of them is hiding their true thoughts and feelings. As I always say, if two or more people are talking and no one ever disagrees, someone is lying. However, regardless of whether you are arguing with your boss, a teammate or your significant other, there are a few things you can

> **❝**No one can argue with how you feel. They **can** argue whether they are or are not making you feel that way. **❞**

say that will immediately turn the conversation into a defensive, no-win situation. It will then escalate out of control, people will say things they regret (thank you, Emotional Brain), creating hurt feelings and grudges, and the problem may go on for days, months or even years. Avoid using these five phrases and you will have a much greater chance of having a reasonable conversation about informational differences, developing and implementing a solution and resolving the problem.

"You make me.... (angry, mad, crazy, etc)"

No one makes you anything. You get to chose. By telling someone

> **❝**If two or more people are talking and no one ever disagrees, someone is lying. **❞**

they make you feel a certain way you are giving them your power. If they could make you something they would likely just make you agree with them and be done with it. When you have feelings during a disagreement, own them: "I am angry." "I am frustrated." No one can argue with how you feel. They *can* argue whether they are or are not making you feel that way.

"It is your fault...."

Placing blame never accomplishes anything. Once there has been an accusation of blame the conversation will become a back-and-forth argument that escalates about who is at fault rather than being a reasoned discussion about the problem and how to solve it.

"You are.... (stupid, lying, wrong, etc)"

A personal attack will immediately put the other person on the defensive and the discussion becomes win/lose. Instead, try to keep the lines of communication open by controlling your side of the conversation: "My recollection of the facts are different." "That is not how I remember it." "From my perspective...." "I understand your point. This is where I disagree...." Your Emotional Brain may believe someone is lying or stupid. Your Logical Brain needs to edit that information out before it comes out of your mouth.

"You should/shouldn't have...."

Things that happened in the past cannot be undone. Telling someone what they should or shouldn't have done is looking backwards. Instead, look forward. "In the future I would like to see XYZ handled differently." You can discuss why someone made the decision they did or what lead them to take a certain action. But then talk about how they can look at a similar situation differently and what you would like to see happen in the future. Don't "should" on yourself or anyone else.

"You aren't listening to me!"

This is a statement almost guaranteed to be made in any heated disagreement. What is usually meant is "I am not feeling heard." Or "You are not seeing things my way." Or "You are not taking the action I expect you to be taking." Or "I am not getting what I want." It is quite possible that someone is listening to you just fine and they disagree. It is also quite possible that *you* are not feeling heard. You will be more successful in getting your message across if you can say "I am not feeling heard. Can we take a minute and just let me make this point?" or "My expectation was XYZ action."

> **❝Don't "should" on yourself or anyone else. ❞**

Choosing the right words is only half the battle. You can derail an otherwise productive conversation by using all the right words but adding a tone, inflection or body language that doesn't match. Having Productive Conflict™ takes effort but the outcome is so, so worth it.

Now you know the five key phrases that are the bane of healthy, Productive Conflict.™ Up next: Tips on how to have even the toughest conversations. DR

Thought Starters ( )

Which of the five things you should never say in an argument does your Emotional Brain like to use?

_____

_____

_____

In your experience, what has been the reaction from the other person when you have used one of them?

_____

_____

_____

How do you respond when someone says one of them to you?

_____

_____

_____

7 Ten Tips for Having Tough Conversations

There is never a shortage of poorly handled disagreements in the news. From athletic coaches verbally and physically abusing players to executives lying to employees and shareholders, it seems everyone is looking for an easy way to hide from tough conversations. It makes me wonder, where are we supposed to learn the skills we need to successfully resolve a problem? I have never seen Conflict Resolution 101 on a college course list. Parenting books don't have a chapter called "Teaching your child how to have a professional disagreement." Nope, we are all just stumbling through life trying to figure it out.

Since the vast majority of us have never had any training in how to address and resolve miscommunication and disagreement, situations often become a complete hodgepodge of ignoring a problem, talking in circles or screaming at each other. People leave teams, quit jobs, alienate family and end marriages because of unresolved conflicts. You would think that something so vital to success would be taught all the way through school and beyond.

If you know nothing else, these ten tips will set you on the right path:

Know exactly what you want to talk about

> **❝Parenting books don't have a chapter called "Teaching your child how to have a professional disagreement."❞**

The whole point of this first step is to keep you from kitchen-sinking and to help you keep the other person on track. If you don't know where you are going, you are unlikely to get there. When you go into a tough conversation only half-prepared, your Caveman Brain is going to feel a lot more threatened and it is going to be much easier for your Emotional Brain to sidetrack your Logical Brain.

Don't ambush the person

Nobody wants to be called out in a public setting or without time to prepare. You have been thinking about this issue and the conversation you want to have for a long time. The person you need to talk to has been going through life happy-go-lucky, thinking everything is fine. Find somewhere private you can talk. Start with something like, "I have a concern I'd like to chat about. Is now a good time or can we schedule something later today?"

Keep your cool

We have talked about how your Emotional Brain can flood your Logical Brain with neurotransmitters and override it. To keep that from happening, your Logical Brain needs to heed your body's warning system. The key is to recognize your Caveman Brain's signals that a situation is about to get out of control. Does your heart beat out of your chest? Maybe you feel hot or flushed. Some of my clients have reported their stomach or shoulders being tight. This is your fight-or-flight response and only you know what yours is. Make a note of it. When you feel it happening you will know you need to take a breath, bite your tongue and give your Logical Brain a chance to process what is happening to make good decisions.

Actively listen (more on this in the next chapter)

"Oh, but in the heat of a disagreement it is *so* much more fulfilling to talk!" Yes, I know. But if you are always talking or thinking about what you want to say, how will you ever understand what the other person needs or wants? Give the person space to talk and explain their side of things. Listening to understand (not just so that you can respond and disagree) will do two things: One – allow you to determine where you have common ground; and Two – give them a chance to vent their frustrations and become calm enough to have a conversation rather than a confrontation.

> **❝**Collective reality is likely to be different from your individual perception. **❞**

Share your story, don't tell theirs

You've heard the line "If I wanted your opinion I would tell it to you." This happens when a sentence starts with the word "you." When someone interrupts you, rather than saying "You're not listening to me!" try "I'm not feeling heard." Share your thoughts, ideas, feelings and observations as first-person opinions starting with the word "I," rather than as facts. Keep in mind that the collective reality is likely to be different from your individual perception.

Ask for their perfect solution

Who knows, you just might be able to give them what they want. Of course you might think their solution is completely ridiculous and unreasonable. But hear them out. And avoid rolling your eyes.

> **❝**Knowing how to have the tough conversations nobody wants to have will give you a huge advantage in the rat race; whether you are running your own business or climbing the corporate ladder.**❞**

Share your solution

Keep in mind, the reverse of the above comment applies.

Be gracious while sticking to your need for resolution

Hey, I never said Productive Conflict™ is always easy. If they become defensive, roll with it. "I can understand that you would be upset about this. It is an awkward conversation for me, too. I feel like it is better for us to talk about it now rather than stew about it until we are screaming at each other."

Take a time-out

There is no law that says every disagreement must be solved in a single conversation. Recognize when things are escalating to the point of going in circles or stagnating and take a break. Don't just walk away. Let the other person know that you feel like the conversation isn't making progress toward resolution and suggest a time to come back to the topic when you have both had time to cool down.

Find common ground and implement

This will likely require compromise on both sides. As you listen, keep your Logical Brain engaged and look for even the tiniest ideas where you agree. They will be the foundation for resolution. It is much easier to find a winning hand when all the cards are on the table.

Talking about and understanding how to engage in Productive Conflict™ resolution is much easier than actually doing it in a real situation. Like any other skill, it requires practice. I have done whole workshops that focus on helping my clients with these ten steps, and it is typical (and wise) to go over them again in refresher sessions. Don't be too hard on yourself if you have to remind yourself of them several times. Knowing how to have the tough conversations nobody wants to have will give you a huge advantage in the rat race, whether you are running your own business or climbing the corporate ladder.

If you are in the middle of the tough conversation how can you make sure the other person knows you are listening and understand what they are trying to tell you? Turn the page to find out. DR

Thought Starters **( )**

Consider the areas in your life that could benefit from Productive Conflict™ then use the ten tips from this chapter to prepare yourself to have the conversation you need to have.

_____

_____

_____

How do you feel about having that conversation? Is your Caveman Brain causing your fight-or-flight response?

_____

_____

_____

Using the feeling words list in the appendix, what feelings is your Emotional Brain sending?

_____

_____

_____

8 Hearing, Listening, Understanding and Acting

There is a difference between hearing, listening, understanding and acting. Being aware of those differences and how they interact together will help you navigate the treacherous waters of disagreement.

The Basics

Hearing – The vibration of sound waves against the eardrum.

Listening – The conscious act of paying attention to sound.

Understanding – The interpretation of sound into thought that is congruent with the intent of the sender.

Acting – Engaging in a behavior that lets the sender know you heard, listened and understood.

· · · · · · · · ·

You are sitting in traffic. Your favorite radio station is on and you are trying to remember what you were going to pick up at the grocery store. Suddenly you hear a siren (hearing). You turn down the radio, tilt your head and determine the sound is coming from behind you (listening). You look in your mirror and see a fire truck barreling down the middle of the road as cars squeeze to the shoulders (understanding). You move your car to the right to get out of the way (acting).

What we do when we encounter an emergency vehicle on the road is the perfect example of the difference between hearing, listening, understanding and taking action. It is the taking action piece that proves we hear and understand what the siren means. The exact same steps are necessary during a disagreement. Unfortunately, we are not as adept at these steps when we interact with other people and try to persuade them toward our agendas. We can hear but not be listening (like when you are watching your favorite TV show and your significant other is talking *at* you). We can be listening but not understand (like when I tried to tell a young actress in NYC what I do for a living and she responded, "I don't know what any

> **❝** *There is a difference between hearing, listening, understanding and acting. Being aware of those differences and how they interact together will help you navigate the treacherous waters of disagreement.* **❞**

of those words mean"). And we can understand but not take action (like when you ask your coworker to provide you with project data and you never hear back from them). If any of the four pieces are missing, the communication fails.

> **"***If I have to think about what I want to say while the other person is talking, who is listening?***"**

During a disagreement we are usually so busy trying to make sure the other person understands and agrees with us that we forget to listen and make sure they feel understood in return. When everyone is talking and no one is listening, nothing is going to be accomplished. Fortunately we have some control over the direction the conversation takes.

Silence is Golden

If you are a Type A, highly driven person like I am, you likely view silence as a waste of time. Nobody is saying anything, thoughts and ideas are not being shared and, therefore, nothing is getting done. Even if you aren't quite that intense about it, silence likely makes you uncomfortable. I am reminded of a boy who was asked to hold a moment of silence for a fallen friend. After about fifteen seconds the boy said, "Okay, that's enough." The crowd chuckled. I know exactly how the boy felt. Silence is intimidating.

Pay attention the next time you are in a discussion. How much silence is there? I would bet almost none (unless someone is giving the silent treatment, which is a different problem). I pose this question: If someone is always talking, when is anyone supposed to think? The only possible answer is, while someone else is talking. Now, if I have to think about what I want to say while the other person is talking, who is listening?

Ahh, now we see the problem. No one is listening because someone is always talking and everyone else is thinking about what they want to say. No wonder we can't communicate!

An additional thing to consider is that it takes people different lengths of time to formulate what they want to say. If you are a person who is always filling the silence, more "polite" communicators will never have a chance to have their voices heard. Conversely, if you are someone who has trouble speaking up when someone else is talking, you could certainly benefit by asking the people you interact with the most to allow for a little more silence in a conversation.

You Can't Observe Why

If you have ever interacted with a toddler, you know their favorite question is "Why?" Parents will tell you they are asked this question a million times a day. That is because toddlers realize it is impossible to know the answer unless you ask. Unfortunately, as we grow up we are taught that asking why all the time is annoying and we stop doing it. That doesn't mean the curiosity goes away. We still want to know. But instead of asking, we start

> **❝**If you are a person who is always filling the silence, more "polite" communicators will never have a chance to have their voices heard. **❞**

making up why people do or say things. As adults our reflex to make up reasons why becomes so practiced we don't even realize we are doing it. Do you recognize yourself in the following example?

· · · · · · · · ·

A few mornings ago I was sitting at an intersection when I saw a mid-size pickup run a red light. Not a just-went-from-yellow-to-red red light. A had-been-red-so-long-I-didn't-see-it-change red light. Luckily for the pickup driver the person with the right-of-way was paying attention and hit the brakes as I gasped and my heart rate

> **❝You cannot observe why someone feels the way they do or why they chose to take the actions they did, only the symptoms of those feelings or behaviors – and it is very likely you will misinterpret what you see. ❞**

tripled. I don't think the guy in the truck even realized he was about three feet from having a really, really bad day.

Put yourself in the almost-victim's shoes for a second. If I asked you about your drive to work that morning how would you describe the near-accident? It would likely include something like "This idiot in a pickup almost flattened me!" Part of that sentence is true; you were almost hit by a pickup. But why it happened, the other driver being an idiot, is an assumption.

I am guilty of making up why when people do "dumb" things and I know better. What other reason could there be for that driver running the red light? Actually, there are a million likely reasons that have nothing to do with the guy's IQ. Maybe he just became a new father and is driving home from the hospital exhausted. Maybe he just closed a huge deal and is excited to get home and tell his wife. Maybe he simply wasn't paying attention. Have you ever accidently run a red light, cut someone off in traffic or made a decision that wasn't very safe? I have and I don't think I'm an idiot.

Making up that someone is an idiot is a negative, permanent and personal attribution. The other reasons I listed are neutral, short-term and situation-specific. When we make up reasons why someone does or says something, we tend to make it about them as a person, something they are and always will be (similar to engaging in relationship conflict). But when we think about the why's of our own behavior it is usually situation-specific (an informational difference).

> **❝As adults our reflex to make up reasons why becomes so practiced we don't even realize we are doing it. ❞**

The next time someone does or says something that annoys you, try to catch yourself as you make up the reason why. Instead of inventing "they did that because" out of thin air, ask them. It is amazing what people will tell you if you just give them a chance. If you absolutely must make up something, try assuming something positive or at least neutral. Remember, you cannot observe why someone feels the way they do or why they chose to take the actions they did, only the symptoms of those feelings or behaviors – and it is very likely you will misinterpret what you see.

Don't Confuse the Situation with the Facts

This is absolutely one of my favorite phrases. I bet I say it a least five times a week. My friends and family are so used to hearing it they will just say, "I know, situation, facts." I have mentioned a few times how the Emotional Brain can override the Logical Brain with neurotransmitters and we say things we regret. Confusing the situation with the facts is similar in that the Emotional Brain is running the show but different because the Logical Brain is saying, "I see your logic and I chose to disregard it."

Let me share one of many, many examples I have seen. I am going to pick an extreme one so that you can see the power of the Emotional Brain.

·········

I was hired by a very successful business owner to provide executive coaching. From the outside she seemed to have everything - a big house (kept clean by someone else), nice cars, two wonderful, happy children, a supportive spouse and a thriving business. As I sat in her elegantly appointed office sipping mango iced tea, she talked about an emotional affair she was having with a recently separated "friend." I had known there was something going on in her life that she wasn't telling me. I had even picked up enough clues to be pretty sure it had to do with her marriage.

Over the course of several sessions we talked about the damage this relationship could create; the disruption to her children, the devastation to her husband (whom she herself described as a great guy who loved her and deserved better) and not only what it *could* do to her business, but what it *was* doing. It had become common

71

for her to not show up until late in the day and disappear for hours so that she could spend time with her "friend." Would her high-profile clients want to continue doing business with her and trust referring their friends if/when the affair came to light? It would be scandalous. It could very easily cause her life to come crashing down around her. And for what gain?

Every time we talked about a risk, she would look down, shake her head and say, "I know. I totally know you're right. So why don't I want to stop?"

•••••••••

Put aside your moral judgment about her situation and consider the power of the Emotional Brain. This wasn't a foolish woman with so much hubris that she assumed she would never be caught - or that if she was, there would be no consequences. She was honestly and truly fearful of the repercussions and yet felt powerless to change her actions.

We see this type of behavior with regard to food, sex, exercise, smoking and anything else that we know we "should" do but don't. If the Emotional Brain is so powerful that it can make us do things that could have negative, life-altering consequences, why are we surprised when our logical arguments don't win over a coworker, or when our pointing out the facts doesn't cause everyone to line up behind us and see things our way?

You will know when you have engaged with someone's Emotional Brain because they will say, "Yeah, but…." This means they agree with your logic, but their gut or feelings disagree. Stop throwing facts and logic at them and work to understand their emotions. Once you do you will be able to have a discussion that gets to the root of the decision-making process and determine if change is possible. Sometimes all the logic in the world can't

> **❝The Emotional Brain is so powerful that it can make us do things that could have negative, life-altering consequences.❞**

override emotions. That is why there is nomenclature in our culture about making decisions with our heads (Logical Brain) instead of our hearts (Emotional Brain).

We know that in a disagreement it is important to allow space (silence) so that everyone has time to process what is being said before they respond. We understand that we have to be careful about making up why someone does or says something and that the facts are not as powerful as we would like them to be. Below I have provided seven guidelines for handling a disagreement once it is in process.

Disagreement Guidelines

- **Prepare yourself to listen** – Remind yourself that more than fifty percent of handling a disagreement is understanding the other person's side.

- **Verify your understanding throughout the conversation** – Use sentences like, "Let me make sure I understand...," "What I think you are saying is..." or "It sounds like you are frustrated by...." If your understanding is not quite in line with what the person is trying to tell you, give them a chance to restate themselves.

- **Provide verbal and nonverbal acknowledgement** – Look at the person talking to you and encourage them to continue to talk. Don't interrupt them. The best solutions develop like a painting. You have to know what colors are on the canvas before you add more.

> **❝**Sometimes all the logic in the world can't override emotions. **❞**

- **Do not judge information as good or bad** – If you jump to positive judgment the other person may assume you agree with them and not give you the whole story. It also makes the assumption that you have the right to judge them at all. If you decide the information they are providing is bad, it is easy to stop listening, which can shut down the dialogue or cause the other person to escalate. Managing a disagreement means managing all of your emotions.

- **Summarize their points** – This is the moment when you get to show that you heard the other person and you understand what they told you. Recap your understanding of what you heard before you start your side of the dialogue.

- **Ask what action they would like to see** – You might not be able to give them what they want, but if you don't ask you miss the possible opportunity to easily solve the situation.

- **Ask for them to listen to your side** – There is nothing more frustrating than carefully listening to someone, making sure you understand their side of things and then having them interrupt and talk over you. This is your cue to politely but firmly request that they hear you out.

Now that you understand the power of listening, hearing, understanding and taking action I am going to share a skill it took me a long time to learn: how to make a point without being aggressive. **DR**

Thought Starters ( )

How does silence in a conversation make you feel?

_____

_____

_____

Think of a time when you made up reasons why someone did something. Did you make a negative assumption about the person?

_____

_____

_____

What would your friends, family or coworkers say about you as a listener? How could being a better listener benefit you?

_____

_____

_____

9 The Secret to Making Your Point without Being Aggressive

I am guessing at this point in the book that you will not be surprised to hear that I don't care if you call it "aggressive," "assertive," "dogmatic" or "going on the offensive." I am not a fan of people steamrolling others with ideas, opinions or demands. When I talk to clients about the need for Productive Conflict™ and how being too nice is bad for business I have received comments like this one:

"I get that being too nice limits success because good ideas get buried, bad ideas aren't challenged and customers take advantage of me. But I have seen people latch onto opposing ideas and meetings just deteriorate into ugly standoffs. It makes me want to vow to never to have an opinion about anything. I don't want to deal with the stress."

I don't want to deal with the stress of people arguing and getting nowhere either. Fortunately, there's a way to make your opinions heard without triggering those ugly standoffs.

·········

I was angry. Actually, "seething" might be a better word. I was in a four-way meeting and had just sat and patiently listened as someone changed the conversation from being about the problem we were discussing to being about my personal character. I had several concerns about this tactic. For one thing, we weren't here to talk about me, and my character had nothing to do with the issue at hand. For another, what he had said was completely false. I don't know if his information was incorrect or if he was deliberately lying. But he was absolutely, flat-out wrong.

I took a breath and realized that I had been clenching my teeth. I knew I was going to have to keep a tight grip on my Emotional Brain or this was going to get ugly quickly.

He finally stopped talking and I said, *"Have you covered all the points you needed to address?"* He responded in the affirmative.

My first task was to show that I understood his points about the topic (how he felt about me was not relevant) and get the conversation back on track. As I started talking he interrupted me.

Me: *"Neal.* (He kept talking.) *Neal!* (He kept talking.) *Neal* (firmly over the top of him), *if you want to have a discussion about this topic I am happy to do so. If you are going to be the only one who does any talking, the rest of us will step out and allow you to have the room to yourself."*

Somewhere during that sentence he had stopped talking. I then said, *"I gave you the professional courtesy of allowing you to say what you wanted to say and attack my character without interrupting. If you are unable to maintain your composure so I can respond, we will take a break until you can."*

❝If there was a transcript made of the conversation, would there be hyphens or periods at the end of each person speaking?❞

The rest of the meeting was tense. Several times I had to stand my ground and demand to be heard but I did not have to table the conversation and walk out of the room. Had Neal continued to refuse to allow for a dialogue, I most certainly would have.

· · · · · · · · ·

As we talked about in the last chapter, the first step to keeping your discussions from turning into win-lose face-offs is to hear the other person out. It isn't always easy, and it raises my blood pressure when a conversation becomes hostile. But always start by listening anyway. It gives you the upper hand in the end. Here are the steps I use – and train my clients to use – to maintain composure and keep a conversation productive as long as possible:

Listen first

To summarize Chapter 8: If you are thinking about what you want to say or that the other person is simply wrong, you aren't really listening to their point. It doesn't matter how much you disagree or how wrong you think they are, don't let your emotions run away with you. Take notes on what they are saying if you need help staying focused.

Create a no-interruption norm

If there was a transcript made of the conversation, would there be hyphens or periods at the end of each person speaking? If you listen without interrupting, you have more leverage when you request that someone not interrupt you. Don't be shy about asking for it.

Make it clear that you understand

Start your rebuttal (for lack of a better word) by saying "I understand your key points are…. I have concerns about…." Making it clear that you understand but disagree should help keep the other person from interrupting you to repeat themselves – particularly if they are the type of person who thinks that if you don't agree with them, you must not have heard them and says the same thing, only louder.

Request to be heard

Keeping your cool when someone is trying to escalate a discussion into an argument is challenging. It is also the one thing that will keep the conversation from spiraling into a stalemate. Calmly use statements that show the direction the conversation is going without being accusatory. "I'm getting the feeling you don't want to hear my thoughts." "Nate (using their name makes it personal), I'd like to finish my point so that all the information is on the table for a productive conversation…" Then continue your thought.

Show that you are on the same side

"I know we are both passionate about reaching the best solution. In that spirit, I'd like to continue my point." Don't wait for permission. If the floor was yours, keep going.

End the conversation

This is a bold, last ditch move that is very powerful. "Sue (yes, use their name again), if we aren't here to share and listen to differing opinions in order to make the best choice, there is no reason for us to continue this conversation. I understand where you are coming from and disagree. If you would like to hear my ideas on how I believe we can make a better decision, let's set up time to talk about it again later."

It is *vitally important* that you not be demeaning, patronizing or rude throughout this exchange. The point is not to insult or demoralize the other person; quite the opposite. The point is to have your voice heard and have a meaningful exchange. The entire foundation of creating Productive Conflict™ is listening to and understanding the other person. Doing that first gives you the power to confidently request it in return.

> **❝***If a conversation is going downhill and all of your attempts to bring it back to being productive are thwarted, don't go down with it.***❞**

There is nothing, "mean" or "rude" about owning your power. You don't have to be aggressive or nasty. Stand up straight, raise your emotional shields and say what needs to be said in a kind but firm manner. You are responsible for protecting yourself from emotional and psychological abuse. If a conversation is going downhill and all of your attempts to bring it back to being productive are thwarted, don't go down with it. You always

81

have the power to leave. Always. Even when you are afraid of the consequences.

Standing up for yourself and having a tough conversation in a hostile situation can be very challenging. The other side of the coin is trying to solve a problem with a conflict-avoidant person. How to get that conversation started is up next. DR

Thought Starters ()

When was the last time you had to request that someone not interrupt you? Were you able to do so successfully?

_____

_____

_____

How did your Caveman Brain and Emotional Brain respond?

_____

_____

_____

Were you happy with the outcome? If not, how could you have handled it differently to achieve a better result?

_____

_____

_____

1 0   Productive Conflict™ with a Conflict-Avoidant Person

When I speak about conflict resolution I am often asked, "How do I address a problem with someone who either won't talk to me or agrees with everything I say and then continues to do whatever he or she wants?"

In order to answer that question we need to consider why we sometimes prefer to dodge a problem rather than solve it. I have found that we are motivated by internal factors (our Communication Fingerprint™) as well as external factors (the culture in our organization or norms in our family structure). Consider the following:

We are afraid we will disappoint or anger someone

An employee was asked if he had mailed a contract with the original signatures to an important client. He said he had mailed it. Two days later an envelope stamped "original documents" was seen on the employee's desk, addressed to the client. When questioned, the employee said, "I knew I was going to mail it and didn't want you to be disappointed that I hadn't done it yet."

We are afraid we will get more work

I was standing in the aisle of a large store looking at small appliances. Two employees were restocking shelves and chatting nearby. I didn't hear all of the conversation, but I did hear one of them say, "I know it's a problem. But if I bring it up they are going to give it to me to fix and I'm too busy already."

We believe the leader won't listen to us

Every year the volleyball coach engaged his team in a conversation about who should be captain. After an extensive

> **❝**We need to consider why we sometimes prefer to dodge a problem rather than solve it.**❞**

conversation about the necessary traits and narrowing the list of contenders down to three or four, the coach would do a "heads down vote." He would say each name and count the number of votes by hands raised. Then he would announce who the team had chosen as captain for the next year. He confided in the athlete sharing this story with me that he didn't actually take the vote into consideration. He just let them vote so they felt like they had a say and then awarded the position to the person he wanted.

We have past bad experiences with disagreement

I was working with a young, up-and-coming executive who had been told she needed to be more vocal in sharing her ideas and concerns. Together we discovered her fear of speaking up stemmed from a childhood history of disagreement being met with physical threats and violence.

> **❝**We often mistakenly believe there is malicious intent when someone avoids a difficult conversation. It is more likely that they are anxious and don't want to deal with the disagreement.**❞**

We believe all conflict is "bad"

I asked a 52-year-old why he allowed his coworkers to berate him in front of customers and pawn their paperwork off on him. He responded, "Oh, I just don't want to create waves."

We don't have the skills to successfully handle disagreements

That is why you are reading this book!

Engaging in Productive Conflict™ with a conflict-avoidant person starts with having empathy for why they don't want to do it. We often mistakenly believe there is malicious intent when someone avoids a difficult conversation. It is more likely that they are anxious and don't want to deal with the disagreement. Once we are willing to start from a place of understanding we are better prepared to move the conversation forward.

Bring the issue into the open

Psychologists call this "making the unconscious conscious." Create an opportunity for sharing thoughts and feelings around talking about a topic rather than jumping directly into the problem. In private and without being confrontational, say something like, "It seems like you aren't comfortable discussing XYZ." Then be silent and let them respond.

Avoid being judgmental

Assure them you aren't interested in an ugly conversation or in shaming them; you just want to discuss the issue. I had a friend who complained that her college-age daughter never talked to her about what was going on in her life. But when she talked about her daughter she didn't like her boyfriend, didn't like her major, wasn't fond of her friends and nagged her about staying out too late. Her daughter stopped talking to her because she didn't want to be told everything she was doing was wrong.

Follow up

If someone feels you've ignored them or didn't use their input, they are going to be less inclined to share with you in the future. Even if you have to make a decision that is not in line

> **❝**When we believe that someone agreed to do things a certain way but then didn't follow through, we often feel they are being insubordinate or purposefully difficult. **❞**

with what they shared, go back to them and explain why. Having that knowledge will let them know that you considered their thoughts and ideas and weighed them as part of all the available information on the subject.

One of the most frustrated concerns I hear is, "I asked them to ...,
they agreed, but they keep doing something different!" When we
believe that someone agreed to do things a certain way but then
didn't follow through, we often feel they are being insubordinate
or purposefully difficult. It is possible that is the case. But there are
other possible reasons the situation isn't playing out as expected.
Perhaps they didn't really understand what you wanted, the boss
may have changed their priorities or they simply got sidetracked.

When someone has this frustration I ask them to evaluate the
"agreement" discussion or to play it back for me as they remember
it. What seemed like agreement might be someone voicing
acceptance to get away from an uncomfortable discussion, an
unfinished conversation or maybe the other person felt bullied into
accepting something they weren't really okay with doing. After
assessing how the other person might have perceived the
conversation, you can approach them with one of the following
opening comments:

- I think we might have had different ideas about the outcome
  of our last conversation and I'd like to revisit it.

- I felt like we agreed to... the last time we talked, but that
  doesn't seem to be happening. Can you help me understand
  what is going on?

- I feel like I've been lied to. (Be cautious about your tone if
  you chose to use this one. It can create a defensive response
  and lead to an escalating confrontation.)

I have put these in order from least to most confrontational. Choose the one that best fits your situation. However, make sure you are in a good place emotionally before you approach the person. Never go in with a chip on your shoulder or a sneer in your voice. The conversation simply won't end well if you do.

Of course, there are also situations in which people avoid solving problems because the other person is toxic. Learn how to address toxicity and keep it from dragging you or your team down in the next chapter. DR

Thought Starters ()

Are you more likely to address a problem or avoid it if possible?

_____

_____

_____

The last time you chose not to deal with a problem, why did you avoid it? What was the "cost" for not addressing it?

_____

_____

_____

What can/did you learn from that situation?

_____

_____

_____

11 Dealing with a Toxic Person

I am one of those "nutty" people who manages stress by working out. You can find me in the gym early most mornings. Usually I have a great workout and am ready to attack the day when I leave. But I learned that there is one person I *must* avoid. If Cynical Sally is working out near a piece of equipment I want to use, I find a different way to do my exercise. Never, under any circumstances, do I want to ask how she is or how things are going. In her life, things are always horrible. I would give you examples but I don't want to ruin your day by making you read them. She is like the cartoon character with a perpetual, dark thundercloud over her head and she will share it with anyone who gets too close.

•••••••••

We have all had it happen. You start your day thinking life is pretty good. But after a run-in with Toxic Tommy you suddenly find yourself believing you might be the only intelligent being on the planet. Worse, that negative fungus spreads. Soon everyone around you seems to be bemoaning how horrible things are, how everything is getting worse and how there is no hope for change. Congratulations: You just had a run-in with an energy vampire who is leaching your morale.

> **❝Sometimes we get so accustomed to someone dumping on us that we don't even realize they're doing it.❞**

All is not lost. You do not have to allow Detracting Dan to trash your drive and ideas. You have options. Let's look at how to cope with negative coworkers and clients and how you can protect yourself against the toxic spores of pessimism.

Identify the source

You would think it would be easy to pinpoint. But sometimes we get so accustomed to someone dumping on us that we don't even realize they're doing it. Start paying attention to the people you interact with on a regular basis. Keep track of how you feel when you are in someone's company. Do they always have something to complain about? If you find yourself saying, "Oh, I'm sorry to hear that" or offering other sympathies more than once in a conversation, put yourself on alert. You might be dealing with a toxic person.

Listen to what they have to say

Particularly if it is coworker or an employee. This is counterintuitive. Usually we think we should ignore people who bring us down.

But rather than just listening to how bad they think everything is and agreeing with them, listen to specifically what they are complaining about. Is there anything that could be a legitimate issue that needs to be resolved? It is easy to write off everything as garbage, but it could be nagging problem and you are hearing about it first or often from the "town crier." Ignore the negative emotion for a moment, listen to the content and make them feel heard. Is there something that really needs fixing? Great! That is something you can work with.

> **"**Work toward change on the things you can control, work around or with the things you can't and do your best to ignore people who wallow in trying to do the opposite. **"**

Ask for solutions

If you really have a Negative Nancy or a Miserable Mike on your hands you are going to get more of the "woe is me, there is nothing to be done" attitude when you ask about ideas for solutions. But if you have someone who has not been feeling heard (and therefore keeps repeating the same negative stuff and bemoaning the lack of a solution) they will jump at the chance to develop a plan to make things better. Heaven knows they have thought about it enough to make suggestions.

Take the person aside and talk

Sometimes negative people don't realize the effect they have on other people. Pointing it out and asking them to stop can be very effective. If they are really unaware of their detrimental attitude, find a nonintrusive way to point it out. I once worked with a team that agreed to use the word "stress." When a member of the team started toxic churning, someone would say, "You seem really stressed about that." This was the signal that someone was headed into a negative dive and needed to pull the nose up.

Throw in the towel

If you have tried all of the options and see no improvement, it might be time to accept that you have a toxic person on your hands and that they don't want to change. I worked with a consultant once who said that toxic people needed to be sold happiness somewhere else. "Things are so bad here. No doubt they are better somewhere else. Please go seek them." If you are lucky, your toxic person will move on to "greener" pastures. If it isn't an option to have them move on, avoid them as much as you can.

Inoculation

If Pessimistic Peter or Disparaging Donna don't change and won't leave, and until you can move him or her on, it is important to keep their negativity from affecting you and your team. The best way to do that is to realize what is happening and deliberately decide to not let them bring you down. Talk about it with the people affected. Work toward change on the things you can control, work around or with the things you can't and do your best to ignore people who wallow in trying to do the opposite. When I get caught by Cynical Sally in the gym, I know what is coming. I put up my emotional shields and internally roll my eyes as she tries, unsuccessfully, to drag me into the cesspool that is her story.

Office politics is such a common form of toxicity that I felt it was important to dedicate a chapter to recognizing and handling it. Read on for my tips for dealing with emotional bullying and professional "frenemies." DR

Thought Starters ( )

Do you have a toxic person in your life? What kinds of symptoms are you and/or your team experiencing?

_____

_____

_____

How is the situation being handled?

_____

_____

_____

What would a conversation with them about their negativity sound like?

_____

_____

_____

Keep going!

12 Handling Office Politics

The woman who was supposed to be training me on my new position was sitting in our boss' "office." It wasn't really an office, just a cube with high walls, so I could hear everything being said.

".... She just isn't really that bright. She doesn't get it. I've tried to explain it to her but...." In my mind I could see her shrugging and rolling her eyes.

I don't know how my boss responded but I felt discouraged and stupid. The "training" I was getting didn't seem to be linear in any way. There was so much, "Always do it this way. Except in this case; then do that. But if this happens...." that I was completely lost. I knew this wasn't the first time my coworker had tried to convince someone I wasn't smart enough to do the job.

·········

Most of the office politics situations I have seen and been involved in solving have been cases of emotional bullying (called "relational aggression" by psychologists) – the act of attacking someone's feelings and the relationships they have with other people. Typical outlets for emotional bullying are gossip, rumors and outright lies. Emotional bullying can happen in person, on Facebook and Twitter, via text or in an email. And if you think only teenage girls engage in such behavior, think again. It starts as early as grade school and is rampant in the workforce. How many times have you heard someone say (or even thought to yourself), "Are we still in high school?"

> **❝Emotional Bullying – the act of attacking someone's feelings and the relationships they have with other people. ❞**

Tearing other people down to look like you are building yourself up is how some people level the playing field. And unfortunately, it works. When we hear negative information about someone we *don't know* from someone we do *know*, we believe it. Our Emotional Brain adds content, saying, "This information is from a known source." Rather than taking the time to gather our own data about the other person our Logical Brain takes the easy shortcut and goes with what we've heard. Not very fair, but it is what we do.

It often feels like office politics are outside of our control. It is true that we don't have the power to change what other people are saying. But, we have more control than we think.

100

Learn to recognize emotional bullying

Everyone knows what physical bullying looked like in high school – kids being stuffed into lockers, pushed into walls and generally tormented. Sometimes emotional bullying isn't as in-your-face, so you have to look more closely for it. Ask yourself these questions: In the course of a conversation are you hearing *facts* about a situation or *opinions* about the people involved? Is someone using relationship conflict (I talked about that in chapter 5) to sway your decision in their favor? Hearing things that suggest someone isn't the fastest ride at the amusement park, that they are ugly or not a good person to have on your team are good indicators of emotional bullying.

Don't engage in bullying

I know you are thinking, "Of course I don't bully!" And because you are reading this chapter, maybe you are self-aware enough that you don't. However, double check. Are you ever guilty of pushing your authority to get your way rather than talking something through like you should? Do you talk and laugh with your friends and ignore people you don't know so well (think about networking events)? Do you find the shortcomings of others great fun to share "just for the laugh?" You may think of those types of behaviors like little white lies. "I'm not really hurting anyone." But you are, especially if you are a manager or business owner. You are setting the example that the people under you will emulate. If it is okay for you to talk about people behind their back, your employees will assume it is okay for them to do it too.

Don't allow bullying to take place around you

When we hear someone say something mean, or hateful or tear other people down and we say nothing, our silence is agreement. I am not saying you need to get into a verbal brawl about every bullying statement you hear. But simply saying "That isn't a very nice thing to say" or "I don't agree with that" is enough to make it clear that you do not support what is going on.

> **❝**It often feels like office politics are outside of our control. It is true that we don't have the power to change what other people are saying. But, we have more control than we think. **❞**

Be compassionate

I am not sure when we stopped teaching children how to be kind to one another or when it became acceptable to stomp on anyone and everyone to get ahead. It really isn't that hard to be nice. Check in with people. Ask how they are doing. If you hurt someone's feelings, apologize. I'm hoping mothers still teach this stuff. Use it.

Gather your own information on people

Don't take the shortcut and just go with whatever you hear about someone. Find out for yourself. If it turns out that the person really *is* a jerk, you can be confident that you learned it firsthand, rather than through hearsay. If you can't find out directly, consider other reasons why the situation is occurring. From the example above, my boss was told I wasn't very smart. If he had wanted to consider alternative options, perhaps he would have thought that maybe the training I was getting wasn't very good. Fortunately for me my boss took the laziest of all options. He did nothing – which gave me time to prove that I was smart enough and that the process was more complicated than it needed to be. Our Caveman Brain and Emotional Brain want to take the easy way out. Engage your Logical Brain to get the real truth.

Create guidelines

Enforce the rule that if someone has a problem with someone else, they need to have a conversation about it. I am not saying that as the boss you should never get involved in situations. But don't get drawn into every disagreement. Give the parties the skills to work it out themselves. You are not responsible for having all the answers all the time.

Listen

You will hear the rumblings of emotional bullying. All you have to do is pay attention. Don't ignore "little" things until they are big. Address gossip, rumors and other forms of emotional bullying right away. Make it very clear that such tactics are not okay on your team.

If you are a leader, it is your responsibility to help create a productive work environment. I completely understand that no one wants to play babysitter to a group of adults. However, letting emotional bullying happen because it is easier than coping with it will cause your best talent to leave, undermine productivity and can lead to a hostile work environment.

What to Do When You Are the Target

My boyfriend called and asked if he could pick me up for lunch – a nice surprise, since he very rarely had time for lunch. As I got in the car, he handed me a single red rose (how sweet). I gave him a quick kiss and we headed out to find something to eat.

None of that would be interesting or even noteworthy except that by the time I got back to the office an hour later, one of my teammates (who had been outside when I left)

> **❝**When we hear someone say something mean, being hateful or tear other people down and we say nothing, our silence is agreement. **❞**

had told several people that I was cheating on my boyfriend. She had never met my boyfriend; she had no idea who he was or who had picked me up. She had decided that he could not have been my boyfriend because he had brought me flowers. Apparently she didn't think guys did that for girls they were already dating.

The story became a huge firestorm, with hotspots flaring up constantly. Some people defended me while others argued that it must be true because I "looked like" the type of girl who would cheat. For the ensuing two years I spent in that department, I had to defend myself a couple of times a month.

"Yes, the man who had taken me to lunch was my boyfriend and, yes, sometimes he even brings me flowers."

·········

Even with my education and the years of experience I have in conflict resolution and handling difficult situations, there is one thing that completely eludes me – why people make things up out of thin air and then share them without reservation as if they are facts. The lies that I have heard about myself and those shared from the lives of clients and non-clients alike are shocking. I don't understand the psychology that makes making up a flat-out lie okay.

But, regardless of whether we understand it, there will be times when we become the target of lies and gossip and we need to be able to manage our responses to it. These are a few tips past clients have found useful:

Don't do things that mark you for gossip

You would think this would go without saying, but I receive so many emails and comments on articles I have written that start with, "I had sex with a coworker...," "I took someone's lunch out of the fridge...," "I called in sick and was seen at the lake...," "I got drunk at (pick a party)...," "I spent the night with my boss' daughter, but nothing happened...," "We were just flirting...." I could write a whole book about the tawdry things people do and then ask me how to keep other people from gossiping about it. The best advice I can give is don't do tawdry things.

Talk to the source

Whether it is a complete lie or there is some truth to the story, have a conversation with the person who started it. Don't make it a confrontation. As you learned in Chapter 8, you can't observe why they are talking about it. If you want to know you have to ask them. Who knows what you might learn? It could be that it was just a misunderstanding. It could be that they really are vicious and mean. If so, that is a good thing to know upfront. Perhaps they will even respect your request to stop talking about you.

> ❝ I could write a whole book about the tawdry things people do and then ask me how to keep other people from gossiping about it. The best advice I can give is don't do tawdry things. ❞

Defend yourself judiciously

If you walk around telling anyone who will listen that the rumor is incorrect, you will end up looking like you have something to hide. If someone asks you directly or makes a reference to something being a "fact" or it comes up naturally in a conversation, explain the truth.

Don't assume all whispered conversations are about you

It is easy to get a complex when you feel like everyone is talking about you. Catch your Caveman Brain making up that everyone is out to get you. There are not tigers behind every tree and not every conversation is about you.

Be a happy person

Your life is so much bigger than this one issue. Don't let it consume you. You might want to read Chapter 14 to learn how to keep negative people from owning space in your head.

Involve an authority figure

Emotional bullying could be a human resource issue. If you believe it has gone past the point of being idle chatter and is negatively affecting you personally or your work, it is time to let someone in authority know. If you are the authority figure, it is your responsibility to do something about it. That might mean providing training or even firing the abuser. Do not make the mistake of believing office politics create healthy competition and make people work harder.

Remove yourself from the situation

If you are being emotionally bullied outside of a structured environment such as work or school, it may be time to change your friends. People who are nice to your face and mean behind your back are not people you need in your life. Replace them with people who are kind and supportive and have your best interest in mind.

Life is too short and time is too precious to allow office politics, drama or emotional bullying to steal your potential to succeed. You don't have to accept it as a "part of life" and "some people are just that way." As the saying goes, time flies. The good news is that you are the pilot and you get to decide who gets to be a passenger on My Life Airlines.

On rare occasions you may have to deal with someone who is narcissistic and/or pathologically lies. I hope

❝There are not tigers behind every tree and not every conversation is about you. ❞

> **❝**As the saying goes, time flies. The good news is that you are the pilot and you get to decide who gets to be a passenger on My Life Airlines. **❞**

these cases are few and far between for you. When you encounter a person like that, there is no win/win option. They are always going to do what is best for them with no remorse for the damage or discomfort it causes you. Your only option is to learn from the situation, cut your losses and discontinue all association with that person. Find out more on this in the next chapter. DR

Thought Starters ( )

Consider a time when you were a target of gossip or in a situation rife with office politics. What was the emotional energy on he team?

_____

_____

_____

How do gossip and backstabbing affect your ability to work at your peak?

_____

_____

_____

How are you holding your team accountable to not engaging in office politics?

_____

_____

_____

Stick to it!

13 How to Handle a Power Play

Industrial organizational psychologist Paul Babiak studied 203 executives in 2011 and found that 4 percent where diagnosable psychopaths (an extreme personality disorder). In the general population that number is about 1 percent. If you are dealing with an exceptionally difficult executive, it is possible he or she has a diagnosable personality disorder, like narcissism

I shared a story in the first chapter about a negative situation I had with a narcissistic vendor. You will recall that he tried to thwart a meeting with me and my team to discuss his company's lack of performance by first claiming to only be available for a forty-five minute period that did not fit into my team's schedule, and when that failed, by calling me directly. I was only able to have the meeting I wanted to have by recognizing his power plays and refusing to play his game.

What I didn't include in Chapter 1 are the steps I used to handle the situation. Power plays are so common from clients, vendors and even family members that I am compelled to share the tips that helped me keep my cool and get what I needed out of the interaction.

> **❝**Only respond when you can do so in the way that is best for you, not just your ego. **❞**

Manage your emotional response

When someone pulls a power play, it is easy to allow ourselves to become angry and let our Emotional Brain fire back. Instead, allow your Logical Brain to acknowledge that the other person is trying to play you. Talk it out with a trusted colleague or your business/executive coach. Only respond when you can do so in the way that is best for you, not just your ego.

Focus on what is important

When one of my clients is in a highly volatile situation, I often ask this question: "Is this a hill you are willing to die on?" What I mean is, how important is this one thing to your goal? Can you acquiesce on that point and still get what you want? When my vendor claimed to not be available during any of the times I had provided and gave me a time that didn't work for my team, I had to decide whether it was worth it to force the issue to "make" him meet with us on our timeframe. If I did that, I ran the risk of him delaying the meeting indefinitely. I decided that this wasn't a battle I needed to win and I elected to have my team change their schedules. Don't try to win a power struggle when it will cost you the war.

Don't play their game

Narcissists will do whatever it takes to get their way. Remember, there is no boundary they won't cross. They can bully you, lying about the "facts" until you question your ability to tell the difference between reality and the lies. There is no way you can win if you play their game. Keep yourself grounded in the facts. Write them down if you need to and keep coming back to what you need to get out of the interaction.

Know when to cut your losses

Some things just aren't worth the emotional energy. When a conversation starts to go downhill, don't go with it. Thank the other person for sharing their side of the story, let them know you will get back to them if you need anything more from them, remove yourself from their negative space and decide what your next course of action will be.

> **"Narcissists will do whatever it takes to get their way. Remember, there is no boundary they won't cross."**

You can't save others

When you know someone is a narcissist, it is tempting to try to stop them from abusing other people. But the people you want to help won't always listen. Don't be too hard on yourself if the narcissist's next target doesn't believe you. Their lies were good enough to convince you, and a narcissist can talk their way out of almost anything. You can't change a narcissist or keep them from using the same lies that burned you on other people. Remember, they will walk right though the social and cultural boundaries that keep healthy people from abusing others. They will not change and will stop at nothing to "win."

How to Spot a Narcissist

My first recommendation when it comes to dealing with a narcissist is, just don't! Sadly, they are usually so good at pretending to be nice, good people that you won't know you are dealing with one until they have already taken advantage of you. There are a few behaviors that are bright, red flags begging you to not get involved:

- **They are blame-Teflon** – A narcissist will not accept blame for anything. If you so much as suggest that they might have done something that led to a less-than-stellar result, they will explode. You have never seen someone so angry as a narcissist deflecting blame. If you have a rare occurrence where you have undeniable proof (video might work), they may suddenly go 180 degrees the other way and become a sobbing mess, saying they can "never do anything right" or "the world is out to get them." This is a ploy to change the subject and get you to feel sorry for them.

- **You find yourself saying you're sorry *all* the time** – Since a narcissist is never to blame, the people around them are – and that includes you. You will find yourself always trying to do the right thing and it somehow ends up being wrong. I know of a narcissist who constantly leaves his wallet and keys in his girlfriend's car. It is always her fault when she leaves for work and he is stranded at home. She is expected to drop whatever she is doing and deliver his items immediately. She has apologized so many times for "taking his keys," she's lost count. Her latest defense is to make sure his wallet and keys are on the counter before she goes to bed at night.

> **❝**Pay attention to how often you praise someone in comparison to how often they praise you. With a narcissist, there will be an imbalance. **❞**

- **They have no empathy** – I once watched a narcissist sit at a dinner table next to his sister eating soup while she openly sobbed about having been completely humiliated by her ex-boyfriend. When I pointed out to him that his sister was crying he shrugged and said, "I know." When someone doesn't have the ability to understand and respond appropriately to other people's emotions, be warned. They are likely a narcissist.

- **Oh, they are so nice** – Narcissists are happy to share their stories about being kind, giving people. How they were more than generous in their divorce. How they paid for the extended family to have a night out together. They likely tell the story in an "aww shucks, it was the right thing to do" way. But they are looking for praise. Pay attention to how often you praise someone in comparison to how often they praise you. With a narcissist, there will be an imbalance.

- **They become disproportionately angry** – Minor issues will cause a narcissist to scream, yell, cuss or become sullenly silent. You will never be sure if the next thing you do or say will be the thing that sets them off. You will find yourself questioning absolutely everything. They might ask you a simple question like, "What would you like to eat?" If you answer, "It doesn't matter," you will be in trouble for not having an opinion. If you suggest something, it will be the wrong because it isn't what they wanted. There is no right answer, unless you are somehow lucky enough to guess exactly what they want.

- **You start questioning your own sanity** – If you secretly wish that you could record every interaction you have with someone just so you have proof of what really happened, you may have a narcissist on your hands. I have never had someone who could make me question my memory of even the simplest events like I did when I worked for a narcissist. I honestly thought my memory was going!

- **They tell sad stories to pull you in** – I watched a narcissist reel in multiple women with the story of how his grandfather taught him to read, that at nine he felt lost and abandoned when his grandfather died in his sleep and how horribly distraught he was not to be allowed

> **❝***If you secretly wish that you could record every interaction you have with someone just so you have proof of what really happened, you may have a narcissist on your hands.* **❞**

116

to go to the funeral. Turns out, the family didn't hold a funeral.

> **❝***If you suddenly wake up one day and realize that you have a narcissist in your circle of friends, family or coworkers – run! Run away as fast as you can.*❞

- **They will lie when there is no reason to do so** – One of the biggest challenges with narcissist is that they lie with absolutely no remorse. They are so used to lying that they may not even realize they do it. I heard someone lie to her mother about the weather. When I asked her why she did it, the woman shrugged and responded, "I don't know." I think she wanted her mom to think the weather here was worse than it was there and feel badly for her. Talk about manipulating someone's emotions!

- **They only think of themselves** – After a presentation, a woman came up to me to privately share a story about why she no longer engages in a hobby she enjoys. One Christmas she secretly cross-stitched her husband's initials on the cuffs of a couple of his dress shirts. On the day after Christmas he said he liked it so much that he wanted her to do the rest of his business shirts. After that if he saw her cross-stitching he would ask, "Are my shirts done? Then why are you working on that? I asked you to do something very simple for me. I don't understand why you can't just do it." Her hobby became such a chore that she stopped doing it entirely.

It is hard to spot a narcissist before you are caught in their web of lies and self-promotion. By the time you notice that they are taking advantage of your kind nature, they are using you for their gain and you are being emotionally sucked dry. If you suddenly wake up one day and realize that you have a narcissist in your circle of friends, family or coworkers – run! Run away as fast as you can. You are never going to be "right" in their eyes. The relationship is toxic and abusive. The sooner you recognize it for what it is and stop trying to save it, the sooner you can start your healing process.

If you have been burned by a narcissist, it may haunt you by swirling around in your head. Next I share how to keep people from owning space in your head. Not only have I used it to help clients, I have used it myself to avoid becoming bitter whenever I have been scalded by someone who uses people instead of things. **DR**

Thought Starters ( )

What was your last run-in with a narcissist or person who regularly lied?

_____

_____

_____

What battle scars do you have from that experience?

_____

_____

_____

How do you think those scars affect the way you interact with people now?

_____

_____

_____

14 Keeping Negative People from Owning Space in Your Head

I kept backing away to avoid the splatter of saliva as I was vehemently told the story of an argument that had taken place the day before. I will spare you the curse-laden details. The short of it was, two grown men almost came to blows over how or whether they were going to share a piece of equipment they both needed to do their jobs. The only thing I could think was, "That was 24 hours ago and you are still literally spitting mad? That guy is stealing your time. Let it go!"

·········

Whether it is the person who cuts them off in traffic, a hurtful phone call from a family member or an attack by a boss, many of my clients find themselves rehashing destructive events in their head. It can cause them to lose sleep, snap at their spouse, drag their coworkers into a downward spiral of depressing pessimism and stop progress towards their goals.

Allowing someone to take up space in our head, without so much as paying a cent in rent, severely limits our ability to perform at our peak. Worse, it makes us unhappy. Here are the questions I talk through with clients to help them vanquish the demon of rerunning a destructive event:

What are you feeling?

The first thing you are going to say is "angry." That isn't going to help you. What is *causing* the anger? Do you feel wronged? Disrespected? Treated unfairly? Disappointed? Get in touch with your Emotional Brain and get to the bottom of what is causing your anger to bubble up and take over your life. Using a list feelings words can be helpful. (See the Appendix for the one I use with my clients.)

Is there anything you can do to change the situation?

Maybe you need to have a follow-up conversation, provide an employee with more training or apologize. If there is something you can do to make things better, create a plan to do

> **❝**Allowing someone to take up space in our head, without so much as paying a cent in rent, severely limits our ability to perform at our peak. Worse, it makes us unhappy. **❞**

it. If there isn't, acknowledge that the situation is over and done and that nothing you do is going to change the outcome. Remember, worrying about something you cannot change is like building a bridge you never want to cross to somewhere you don't want to go.

Have you shared the experience with someone who can help?

When we are angry, we often want to tell people who will share our righteous indignation. But they only wind us tighter and help us build our anger. Instead, talk to someone with a calm head who will help you work through the problem and dissipate your anger.

> **❝**Worrying about something you cannot change is like building a bridge you never want to cross to somewhere you don't want to go. **❞**

What can you learn?

Every situation offers the gift of experience. Take the time to figure out what there is to be gained from the circumstances, even if it only serves as an example of what not to do. Once you cool down you can share it with mentees to help them learn from the event so that they don't have to make the same mistake.

What will you do differently next time?

There is no doubt another disagreement or problem is in your future. Instead of just rehashing a past problem, take the time to articulate how you want to handle things differently in the future. The process of thinking through it will help your Logical Brain remember when your Emotional Brain is once again running in high gear.

Write it down

Sometimes our Emotional Brian wants to keep bringing up something our Logical Brain has already marked "complete." If you have gone through the above steps and are still having trouble

123

letting it go, go through them again. Only this time, write your answers down. I find it most cathartic to do it longhand with a regular No. 2 pencil. For you it might be on your computer, tablet or other device. The point is to create "hard" evidence for your Emotional Brain that the situation is as resolved as it is going to get and to let it go.

I've said this before and I think it bears repeating here: Life is too short to allow negative, mean or hurtful people to steal your time. Don't let them be passengers on My Life Airlines. Decide whether you need to forgive and forget or get over it, but remember it so that it doesn't happen again. Keep reading to learn more about how to do that. **DR**

Thought Starters ( )

What event keeps playing in your head even though you have tried to banish it? What would you do differently next time?

_____

_____

_____

Is there something you handled well and want to do again?

_____

_____

_____

What follow-up needs to be done for the event to be complete?

_____

_____

_____

15 | Forgive & Forget or Burn Me Twice

It has been said that to forgive is a virtue; to forget, sainthood. But "burn me once shame on you, burn me twice shame on me" also rings true. Which is the right answer in the competitive business world? It depends on the situation; and knowing when to apply which rule requires wisdom.

·········

I turned my phone on as we taxied across the tarmac. I had gotten a lot of work done on the two-hour flight and I was feeling like things were in a good place for the upcoming long weekend. Maybe I would even take an extra day off.... My phone buzzed that I had voicemails and I absentmindedly looked down at the screen. There were four calls from a CEO I had created a proposal for about six months ago. I decided I wasn't going to try to listen to them in the noisy plane and switched over to my email. Two emails from the same guy. I had only been in the air for two hours. What could be that urgent?

It turned out that their senior director of sales had unexpectedly quit a couple of months before and a huge potential client she was working on had been handed to Joe, another senior person in the company. Joe had never done direct sales with a client but he knew the product his company offered really well. At the time, everyone agreed he was the best option the company had to finish the proposal and pitch it to the client. Unfortunately, he didn't have the knowledge or the skills to land a client who was now skittish because their contact left without warning and the project was awarded to a competitor.

> **❝***Only the most experienced closer can be expected to walk on in the ninth inning of a tight game and come out with a win.***❞**

Several members of the executive team were now finger-pointing and the blame was landing squarely on Joe. He had blown the best opportunity the company had had to hit its numbers that year. One of the C-suite executives had even said he would "never trust Joe to come through in a crunch" again.

Joe felt like he had been hung out to dry by being dumped into a high-pressure situation and not given the resources or the support he needed to be successful.

The team was being torn apart and they weren't going to get *any* new clients if they couldn't get back on track and show a united front.

Is this a situation where Joe "burned" the team and they are justified in not trusting him with big projects, or is this a time to forgive and forget? In this case I said, "forgive, train, and retest." Joe did not intentionally or maliciously lose a big contract. He was thrown into an unlikely-to-win situation. Only the most experienced closer can be expected to walk on in the ninth inning of a tight game and come out with a win. Joe and the team needed to move past this client (forget) and look to the future. If Joe was going to be expected to jump in and close big deals he needed to accept that he didn't know how, get the training he needed and be given opportunities and support to succeed; not banned from ever working with customers again.

·········

Have you seen the cell phone commercial where a man and woman are talking about a phone that can do two things at once? The woman says "You can watch videos *and* text." The man replies, "Or you could watch the earnings report and take notes like we are supposed to." She rolls her eyes and asks for his notes. With a touch of their phones she has his work. When a third person (presumably the boss) walks up and asks if either of them put together the earnings report, the woman is quick to raise her hand and say she did.

·········

What do you think, forget or burn? In this case I would say learn from being burned. The woman intentionally manipulated the situation for her benefit and to the detriment of her teammate. If you have someone like that on your team, you may have to collaborate with them, but you don't have to let them walk on you. Keep good records of your ideas and be careful about open brainstorming sessions where they can use you. Don't forget, professional skepticism is the way to go. If they do it again, you can't say you hadn't been warned.

An engineer once said to me, "It is easy to learn who someone is. It is hard to remember." If you are forgiving and trusting by nature, it may take being burned by the same person multiple times to remember you can't "forgive and forget" with them. If you are more of a "one strike and you're out" person, you may have a really hard time letting go of a small infraction by someone who is actually a great teammate. To find middle ground, you need to know which way you lean and take the time to allow your Logical Brain to sort through the information your Emotional Brain is sending. I encourage clients to honestly explore if the situation was caused by a genuine mistake or if it was a selfish, malicious act. It is also helpful to understand the difference between and explanation and an excuse.

An Explanation or an Excuse?

I had an appointment with a very important client and needed to bring on a consultant for some expert work. I reached out to my network and three different people recommended the same consultant for doing the highest quality work in the area. One

❝It is easy to learn who someone is. It is hard to remember.❞

person did give a caveat – yes his work was good, but he was notoriously late for everything. I scheduled an exploratory meeting with him. He was ten minutes late. But he knew his stuff and he had a better track record and professional presence than anyone else I could find. Before I brought him on board I explained my reputation for being prompt. Respecting my clients' time was very important to me and something I was known for in my field. Being late for this meeting was not an option. He said he understood and suggested I meet

> **❝**I encourage clients to honestly explore if the situation was caused by a genuine mistake or if it was a selfish, malicious act. **❞**

him at his office forty-five minutes before the appointment and that we make the thirty-minute ride together. That way there was no way he could get "caught-up" in something and be late. My anxiety about his tardiness was assuaged, the recommendation for the quality of his work overrode my concerns and I engaged his services.

The day of the meeting I arrived at his office only to be told by his receptionist that he had not yet returned from his previous appointment. I was a little early (as is my norm) so I sat down to wait. Forty minutes later he came rushing in full of apologies. He grabbed his paperwork and proceeded to drive like a crazy person to my client's office. We were, of course, late.

On the ride back to his office he launched into how he had an appointment that he had been trying to schedule for the last six months. He knew when he made it he was going to be tight for time with me but he thought he could make it. It ran longer than he had expected and that wasn't his fault. At which point I asked him, "And the meeting with my client was the least important thing

131

you could think of to schedule over in the last six months?" He responded, "I am just trying to explain." And I said, "It isn't an explanation, it is an excuse and I don't need to hear it."

·········

When a mistake is made, an explanation is provided to clarify what happened, why it was a onetime slip-up and why it won't happen in the future. An excuse is a song and dance to justify what happened with no plan or expectation to change. If you are really getting an explanation and an apology, accept it and move on. If you are getting an excuse, take it with a grain of salt. The underlying message might be similar to the Tracy Byrd song, "I'm not sorry. I'm not wrong and it's probably going to happen again."

Fortunately, because of my usual promptness my client forgave me for being late. However, I have no intention of using that consultant again.

When we feel like we need to explain, we probably also need to apologize; because we can't use Ctrl-Z to undo life's mistakes.

When You Wish Life Had an Undo Button

There is going to come a time when you say something you wish you hadn't or flat-out make a mistake. You could

> **❝**An explanation is provided to clarify what happened, why it was a onetime slip-up and why it won't happen in the future. An excuse is a song and dance to justify what happened with no plan or expectation to change. **❞**

ignore it. But you know it won't go away. You could give one of those sorry-if-I-maybe-did-something-you-took-the-wrong-way non-apologies, which is likely to make the situation worse, not better. Or you can do the professional thing, own up and apologize.

Reasons (other than it being the right thing to do) why apologizing is the way to go:

- **It shows the damage has stopped and rebuilding can start** – When you're on the receiving end of hurt, hearing "I'm sorry" indicates it is safe to come out of hiding and start the healing process.

- **It accelerates the resolution process** – There is nothing that says I am ready and willing to fix this like taking responsibility.

- **It is the medicinal balm on an emotional injury** – Fortifying a marred connection means owning your mistakes.

Do it right:

- **In person** – Don't hide behind email, text messages or even the phone. Apologize face-to-face or at least via video so they can see your eyes.

- **In kind** – If the slight was in public, apologize in public. It is unfair to cause hurt publicly and take responsibility for it privately.

- **Forgo the explanation** – You may have had the best intention and it went awry. But this is not the time to justify.

- **Show that you understand what caused the hurt** – Remember when you were little and your parents made you apologize?

You would say "Sorry!" and they would say "For....?" (At least that is how it happened in my family.) Make sure you include what you are apologizing for.

- **Make it right** – If you broke a window, you would have pay to fix it (like I did when I was 11). If possible, make restitution. For emotional mistakes, ask what would make it right.

- **Don't do it again!** – Saying I'm sorry carries the implicit understanding of saying "I know what I did was wrong or hurt you and I won't do it again." Making the same "mistake" again and again and apologizing again and again is indicative of an abusive relationship.

The good thing about apologizing is that once that tough conversation is over, you have a line in the sand delineating life before the incident and after. If it is brought up again by someone who is kitchen-sinking you can say something like, "When we discussed that and you accepted my apology I considered it finished."

On a final note, if someone offers you an apology, accept it. If they feel the need to explain (not make an

> **❝**If the slight was in public, apologize in public. It is unfair to cause hurt publicly and take responsibility for it privately. **❞**

excuse) listen. You don't have to forget but there is no point in holding a grudge and looking for retribution or justice. Doing so only means they are taking up space in your head without paying rent.

Handling disagreements and making things right isn't always in your hands. Sometimes you have to rely on your employees. If they aren't properly trained they can ruin your hard-earned brand reputation in microseconds. How it happens and what to do about it, next. DR

Thought Starters ❨❩

Are you more likely to hold a grudge or allow the same person to burn you more than once? Why? What factors do you take into consideration?

_____

_____

_____

Do you often feel the need to "explain" as part of an apology? Why do you think that is?

_____

_____

_____

Is there a situation in your life that needs to be addressed and an apology made? What is keeping you from taking care of it?

_____

_____

_____

Preventing Your Employees from Damaging Your Brand

This story was shared with me by a woman I will call Jayne. This is a summary of two phone calls with her doctor's office and the fallout that followed:

Doctor's staff person: *They found two abnormalities. You need to come in for a follow up visit now. Your regular doctor is on vacation next week. I can book you with her partner or you can see your doctor a week from Monday.*

Jayne: *Is this issue urgent enough that I need to see her partner or can I wait until my doctor is back?*

Staff person: *I don't know.*

Jayne: *Ummm, okay. What else can you tell me about the results?*

137

Staff person: *That's all the doctor wrote.*

Jayne: *What else is on the report from the lab?*

Staff person: *You will have to talk to the doctor about that.*

Jayne: (frustrated) *Please book an appointment for me with my doctor on the day she returns and have her partner call me back today.*

Staff person: *Okay. Her partner won't be able to call you until tomorrow.*

Jayne: *That is fine. Please just make sure she calls me.*

> **❝Once you have trained your employees how to handle disagreements with each other and with customers, you will have policies and guidelines in place to which you can hold them accountable. ❞**

The next day Jayne called the doctor's office at 10 a.m.

Jayne: *Hi, I left a message yesterday for Dr. XYZ to call me today. Can you tell me what time she might call? I want to make sure I don't miss her.*

Staff person: *The doctor will not be calling you. She is busy seeing patients today. If you have questions you need to make an appointment.*

Jayne: *I already have an appointment for next week with my doctor. I just need to ask a couple of questions to clarify the information I was given.*

Staff person: *The doctor will not be calling you. Make an appointment if you want to talk to her.*

This conversation escalated to the point that Jayne hung up, got in her car and drove to the office to explain (loudly in front of other patients) that the doctor and her staff were not God, they did not get to make unilateral decisions about her health and if the doctor could not give her five minutes of her time to answer a couple of simple questions they could make a copy of her file and she would find another doctor immediately.

The good news is, Jayne did receive a call and get her questions answered. The bad news, she is still thinking about looking for another doctor; even though she really likes her doctor and has been going to her for almost ten years. I wonder how many people's health has been negatively affected by this doctor's staff and how many patients have left without saying anything.

·········

It doesn't matter how amazing your clients think *you* are. If your employees are treating them badly, they will take their business somewhere else. Here are a few things I have found that increase the odds that the people you have working for you are treating your clients, customers or patients well:

Remember, *it* rolls downhill

How you treat your employees is how they will treat your customers. Think about that the next time you are talking to them. Would you speak to a customer the way you are speaking to your employees?

Productive Conflict™ is a teachable skill

If you want employees who are empathetic and able to listen to your customers' concerns, even when they hear the same complaint fifty times a day, provide them with the skills to do so. The amount you spend hiring a competent consultant for a workshop and the continued development

> **❝**Your employees are the face of your business. They have ultimate control over whether your customers leave happy or leave angry. It only takes a second to lose a customer. How much time and marketing budget will it take you to find a new one?**❞**

of your staff will be made back exponentially when your customers feel appreciated and heard (even when you can't always give them what they want).

Toxic employees will kill your business

Once you have trained your employees how to handle disagreements with each other and with customers, you will have policies and guidelines in place to which you can hold them accountable. For every customer who takes the time to complain, there are between seven and ten who just walk away. If you have an employee who repeatedly treats your customers poorly, even after training, you don't need them interacting with your customers. They are clearly not a good fit for your business.

Address problems individually

When I worked in customer service, my manager would berate

the whole team when there was really only one employee who had a problem. I remember feeling abused because she was hurtful, saying things like "Since you all haven't figured this out yet (insert eye roll), I will go over it *again*." I did get it and didn't appreciate my time being wasted because she didn't want to have a one-on-one conversation with the problem person. Step up to the plate and have the tough conversations.

Your employees are the face of your business. They have ultimate control over whether your customers leave happy or leave angry. It only takes a second to lose a customer. How much time and marketing budget will it take you to find a new one? Can your business really succeed with a revolving door of customers?

How disagreements with customers are handled is part of your company culture. The culture you have was either built, created or allowed. In the example below they allowed a culture of trying to hide problems rather than addressing them.

Lessons from Dreadful Customer Service

A vehicle was brought to a dealership for warranty work. It took longer than expected and the dealership kept the vehicle over the weekend. They then proceed to park it, outside in the pouring rain with the side window removed. They called to say the vehicle was ready on Wednesday, totally failing to mention the water issue.

When the customer got home she noticed the entire passenger floorboard was soaked. When she called the dealership, they admitted that they'd left it parked outside with the passenger window sitting on the roof, but promised to "make it right." Ten days later, after claiming the carpet was dry on three separate occasions, being proven wrong, asked multiple times to replace the carpet, and saying "no, we'll just dry it out," there were still puddles of water dripping into the storage area under the seats. Can you imagine the state of the wiring running

> ❝A mistake is an opportunity to realize a protocol needs to be created to avoid the issue in the future. ❞

under the carpet, the rust starting to form at every connection point? What about the smell in the summer as the car sits in the hot sun and mildew flourishes in the padding? I certainly wouldn't want to be in that car.

· · · · · · · · ·

I don't know what the outcome of this shoddy customer service story was. But it does provide a backdrop for us to look at our own businesses and the wrong way to handle a customer problem. Let's dig a little deeper:

- The technician who left the window out told his direct superior when he realized his mistake, but it went no further up the chain. If an employee in your organization reports a customer problem, **do you have protocols on how that information is handled?**

- There was no mention of the water when the customer picked up the vehicle. Instead, the dealership left it to soak through her pants as she knelt to unbuckle her child's safety seat. What is keeping your employees from pretending a

142

problem doesn't exist? **Do you have plans in place to make sure bad news makes it to the top?**

- When the customer pointed out the problem the manager shook her husband's hand, looked him in the eye and said "we'll make it right." They proceeded to do everything in their power to fake it well enough that the customer would just go away. **Do your employees have the authority to really fix a problem rather than just putting a patch on it and hoping they can get away with it?**

- The customer was told that the technician who made the mistake would be personally responsible for covering the cost of the repairs. Sharing this with the customer was a bullying tactic; trying to use guilt to get away with damaging personal property. It also may explain why they were trying to take the cheap route rather than the correct one. **Do your office policies place blame rather than provide training?** A mistake is an opportunity to realize a protocol needs to be created to avoid the issue in the future. Your internal protocols, or lack thereof, are not your customer's concern.

- The dealership's general manager wouldn't return phone calls and was nowhere to be found on the multiple occasions the customer went to the dealership since the debacle started. **When a customer has a problem, do you hide behind your staff?**

Clearly the reputation of this dealership has been damaged. If this customer decides to share the story with the local news station or post the complaint online, what is now an issue with one customer could turn into a public relations nightmare.

There a few very clear lesson to learn here:

- Create a culture in which mistakes are aired, not buried.

- Train your employees to solve problems the right way, right away.

- Avoid punishing employees for mistakes. It creates a culture of fear.

- Be in the know. You can't help solve a problem you don't know about.

- Establish protocols so that your employees have the knowledge they need to make good decisions when interacting with a customer.

- Don't give your customers reason to drag your brand through the mud.

- Hold employees accountable for creating a positive customer experience.

- Provide ongoing training. Invest in a professional to improve your customer experience.

•••••••••

Even when you can't give customers exactly what they want, it is possible to make them happy. This example is from the comments section of my website, www.DrRobynOdegaard.com:

I was in the grocery store looking for some kind of sugar-free cinnamon bun product or sugar-free oatmeal raisin cookies. I asked an employee who happened to be in the aisle whether the store carried any. She directed me to an aisle where she thought they would be, but she wasn't sure if the store carried them.

> **❝How disagreements with customers are handled is part of your company culture. The culture you have was either built, created or allowed. ❞**

While I was in that aisle looking and not finding them, a manager approached me. He said, "Sugar-free cinnamon bun or sugar-free oatmeal raisin cookies? Let's see what we can do."

He spent the next fifteen minutes with me looking in the cookie aisle, the frozen bread aisle, the natural food section and the ice cream aisle, taking products off the shelf to see if they were sugar-free, and displaying a great deal of product knowledge and creativity. Although we ultimately never found it, he came up with the idea of a sugar-free sprout bread topped with raisins, sprinkled with cinnamon and sweetened with agave.

I was thrilled!

And that's not all. After all of the time that he spent with me, he asked if I had found everything I was looking for that day. I said no, actually – I wanted the store brand of plain, fat-free Greek yogurt but only the name brands at twice the price were available. He took a look, made a call, and told me to pick out any other brand of yogurt I wanted and they would charge me the same price as the store brand.

145

When I happily commented to the cashier, I asked if this incredible level of service was a formal part of training or if the store just always hired service-oriented people. He replied, "Probably both … but during training they tell us never to say 'no' to a customer."

·········

Clearly that grocery store has succeeded in creating a culture that expects employees to do their best to make sure customers leave happy.

You now have almost all the pieces to be able to handle every disagreement every time. The only piece you are missing is being able to play brave. Just one more chapter! DR

Thought Starters ()

What are your expectations around how your customers should be treated?

_____

_____

_____

How have you explicitly shared those expectations with your employees and given them the training and skills to meet them?

_____

_____

_____

How are you holding your employees accountable to treating your customers properly?

_____

_____

_____

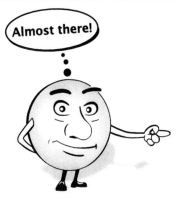

17 Be Brave to be Amazing

You now know how the Communication Corridor™ processes language and why it can lead to misunderstandings and escalating conflict. You understand that each of us has a unique Communication Fingerprint™ that can further muddle an incoming message. You recognize when the Communication Myth™ is in play and you can explain why the Communication Golden Rule™ fails. You appreciate how Productive Conflict™ can make your life better and can identify conflict styles that cause disagreements to escalate. You can tell the difference between relationship conflict and informational conflict and you have oodles of new conflict resolution skills at the ready. All you need now is to put the things you've learned into practice. Sometimes *that* is the scariest step.

In order to win in the game of life you have to be willing to play brave. If you are so afraid of making a mistake that you are paralyzed, you have no chance to succeed. You cannot become

149

effective at Productive Conflict™ unless you practice. You will make mistakes. I still do and I have been using and teaching these ideas for a long time. As entrepreneur Lewis Schiff found in a 2009 national study, how you view failure is a

❝If you are so afraid of making a mistake that you are paralyzed, you have no chance to succeed. ❞

predictor of your future success. Each mistake is a stepping stone. Use your mistakes to gain knowledge to become better at Productive Conflict™.

I will leave you with these ten thoughts to inspire you to play brave:

1. **Play the game that matters to you** – What does success mean to you? I have found that success isn't a thing that is achieved; it is experienced. Perhaps a better question is, what would the experience of success feel like to you? And even more importantly, why does having that experience matter?

2. **Know your goals** – If you don't know where you want to go, you will likely never get there. In handling every disagreement you need to know what resolution looks like to you every time, else you will never be able to achieve it.

3. **Commit to playing offense** – In sports it is apparent that you can't score if you only play defense. In a disagreement you must be willing to stand up for yourself. Reaching resolution requires taking action. If you are always on the defensive, wondering if you should or shouldn't say

something, your competition will run by you. Pick a direction and take it. If it turns out to be wrong, apologize if you need to and change directions.

4. **Invest in yourself** – There are so many lessons you don't have to learn the hard way. Success is often just a matter of learning the right skills from the right person. You must believe that you are valuable and give yourself the ability to ask questions from people who can help you.

5. **Own your power** – When an opportunity arises to use Productive Conflict™ and you stutter-step, ask yourself why and tell yourself the truth. You can't fight a fear you don't understand and if you aren't honest with yourself, who will be? Give yourself permission to take ownership over the situation and the power to do something about it.

> **❝**If your "friends" find humor instead of opportunity in your life challenges, you need different friends. **❞**

6. **Surround yourself with people who engage in Productive Conflict™** – It is hard enough to take the risks required to be successful without having to deal with people holding grudges and making you struggle to figure out what they need or want. Being around people who make good choices, apologize when they need to, learn from their mistakes and drive forward is contagious. Find them and you will motivate each other.

7. **Build a great team** – It is so much easier to play brave and risk making mistakes when you know your team is there to catch you when you stretch just a little too far. Will the people in your life help you up when you fall or laugh? If your "friends" find humor instead of opportunity in your life challenges, you need different friends.

> **❝**Something is only failure if it is the last thing you do before giving up.**❞**

8. **Go for it!** – I believe in strategy, not destiny. Now is the best time to take action.

9. **Evaluate quickly** – Did the action you took move you in the direction of resolution? If yes, do it again. If no, why not?

10. **Be proud of yourself and do it again** – When it comes to Productive Conflict™, once is never enough.

No one has ever been successful by doing nothing. Decisions must be made. Action must be taken. Disagreements must be handled. Something is only failure if it is the last thing you do before giving up.

I have a quote by Mark Twain hanging on my office wall. It reads:

"Twenty years from now you will be more disappointed by the things you didn't do than by the ones you did. So throw off the bowlines, sail away from the safe harbor. Catch the trade winds in your sails. Explore. Dream."

I would add, "Play brave!"

It is my hope that you enjoy much success and that Productive Conflict™ serves you as well as it continues to serve me and my clients.

I invite you to learn more, share your success and submit questions at www.DrRobynOdegaard.com.

Finally and without reservation,

I wish you the MOST from your potential!

APPENDIX

Happy	Afraid	Excited
alive	anxious	alert
cheerful	apprehensive	connected
delighted	desperate	cooperative
ecstatic	fearful	curious
elated	frightened	eager
energized	insecure	energetic
exuberant	intimidated	engaged
fortunate	nervous	enthusiastic
gratified	overwhelmed	inspired
joyful	panicked	involved
loving	scared	nervous
optimistic	shaken	open
pleased	terrified	optimistic
satisfied	unsure	ready
thankful	vulnerable	stimulated
upbeat	worried	thrilled

Unhappy	Confident	Frustrated
alienated	accomplished	aggravated
crushed	capable	annoyed
defeated	competent	confused
demoralized	confident	dissatisfied
depressed	courageous	distressed
disappointed	determined	helpless
disheartened	effective	hindered
distraught	encouraged	irritable
drained	hopeful	irritated
empty	perceptive	let down
gloomy	positive	pointless
hopeless	proud	restless
lousy	secure	stuck
miserable	self-reliant	suffocated
sorrowful	strong	uneasy
submissive	successful	uptight

Calm	Angry	Embarrassed
blasé	agitated	ashamed
careless	betrayed	bewildered
collected	bitter	disgraced
composed	disgusted	flustered
content	enraged	foolish
easygoing	exasperated	humiliated
indifferent	fuming	hurt
lackadaisical	furious	idiotic
laid back	hostile	insulted
levelheaded	mad	let down
mellow	offended	mocked
nonchalant	outraged	mortified
peaceful	provoked	offended
relaxed	resentful	self-conscious
relieved	upset	teased
serene	used	uncomfortable

Tired	What additional words would you add?
apathetic	_____
checked out	_____
detached	_____
disengaged	_____
drained	_____
empty	_____
exhausted	_____
fatigued	_____
jaded	_____
numb	_____
shut down	_____
sluggish	_____
stressed	_____
vulnerable	_____
weary	_____
worn out	_____

About the Author

Dr. Robyn Odegaard (aka "Doc Robyn") is an internationally known motivational speaker, author and consultant. She spent fourteen years working in the corporate world before returning to school to earn her Bachelor of Science degree, *summa cum laude*, Phi Beta Kappa in Psychology from Stony Brook University and her Master's and Doctorate degrees in Applied Organizational Psychology, from Rutgers University and then become CEO of Champion Performance Development. She is an in-demand speaker for corporate conferences and tradeshows and provides teambuilding workshops, executive coaching and executive wordsmithing to executives and business owners. Doc Robyn is a regularly sourced expert on communication and conflict resolution in the media and a monthly contributor to two national publications.

Doc Robyn founded the "Stop The Drama! Campaign," wrote the book *Stop The Drama! The Ultimate Guide to Female Teams* and speaks at colleges and universities across the country to be part of the solution that allows young people to be more prepared for the work world.

Don't miss Doc Robyn's ongoing secrets to achieving the most from your potential through Productive Conflict,™ effective communication, active leadership and powerful teamwork. Get her free newsletter at www.DrRobynOdegaard.com.

Another Title by
Dr. Robyn Odegaard

 The Ultimate Guide to Female Teams

Available from www.StopTheDramaNow.com
And other fine book outlets.

Find Doc Robyn Online

LinkedIn: www.linkedin.com/in/robynodegaard

Twitter: twitter.com/DocRobyn

Facebook: Facebook.com/DocRobynO

Website: www.DrRobynOdegaard.com

Email: DocRobyn@DrRobynOdegaard.com

CPSIA information can be obtained at www.ICGtesting.com
Printed in the USA
BVOW07s1329060913

330351BV00002B/19/P